All Things Beautiful

PATRICK MAGUIRE
with Caeli

Copyright © 2025 Patrick Maguire with Caeli.

All rights reserved. No part of this book may be used or reproduced by any means, graphic, electronic, or mechanical, including photocopying, recording, taping or by any information storage retrieval system without the written permission of the author except in the case of brief quotations embodied in critical articles and reviews.

Balboa Press books may be ordered through booksellers or by contacting:

Balboa Press
A Division of Hay House
1663 Liberty Drive
Bloomington, IN 47403
www.balboapress.com
844-682-1282

Because of the dynamic nature of the Internet, any web addresses or links contained in this book may have changed since publication and may no longer be valid. The views expressed in this work are solely those of the author and do not necessarily reflect the views of the publisher, and the publisher hereby disclaims any responsibility for them.

The author of this book does not dispense medical advice or prescribe the use of any technique as a form of treatment for physical, emotional, or medical problems without the advice of a physician, either directly or indirectly. The intent of the author is only to offer information of a general nature to help you in your quest for emotional and spiritual well-being. In the event you use any of the information in this book for yourself, which is your constitutional right, the author and the publisher assume no responsibility for your actions.

Any people depicted in stock imagery provided by Getty Images are models,
and such images are being used for illustrative purposes only.
Certain stock imagery © Getty Images.

Print information available on the last page.

ISBN: 979-8-7652-6626-7 (sc)
ISBN: 979-8-7652-6627-4 (e)

Balboa Press rev. date: 09/23/2025

Contents

Introduction ix

Chapter 1	Sunset District Irish 1
Chapter 2	Bye, Dad 5
Chapter 3	Revenge List 9
Chapter 4	Carville and the Coffee House 13
Chapter 5	The Promise (If I Saw You in Heaven) 15
Chapter 6	The Deal 17
Chapter 7	At Least I Tried 19
Chapter 8	The First Customer 23
Chapter 9	Miracles & Machines 25
Chapter 10	Against All Odds 29
Chapter 11	Buffy 31
Chapter 12	The Deep Connection 33
Chapter 13	The Road to Grace 35
Chapter 14	The Fall 39
Chapter 15	The Turning Point 43
Chapter 16	The Hard Road to Medjugorje 47
Chapter 17	The Visit 51
Chapter 18	Stress 55
Chapter 19	In God's Hands 57
Chapter 20	Belfast 61
Chapter 21	The Return to The City 67
Chapter 22	Kevin, Our Angel 69
Chapter 23	The Second Blessing 71
Chapter 24	The Cycle of Life 73
Chapter 25	I Know Why the Banshee Cried 77

Chapter 26	The Window	81
Chapter 27	The Fire	85
Chapter 28	Let It Be	89
Chapter 29	Compassionate Friends	93
Chapter 30	The Visitation	97
Chapter 31	Goodbye, Billy	99
Chapter 32	Felix	103
Chapter 33	The Leaf	107
Chapter 34	Hearts & Smiley Faces	109
Chapter 35	The Cottage in Heaven	113
Chapter 36	The Red Shoes	117
Chapter 37	The Stained Glass Gnosis	121
Chapter 38	Ronnie from the Richmond	125
Chapter 39	Toilet Bowl Theology	129
Chapter 40	The Ivory Pagoda	131
Chapter 41	Angels as Animals	135
Chapter 42	Kumusta Ka, My Dear	139
Chapter 43	Forgiveness at S.F. General	143
Chapter 44	House of Pain	147
Chapter 45	The Empty Chair	149
Chapter 46	Collateral Beauty	153
Chapter 47	I Got My Peace	157

Epilogue	163
A Note from the Author	165
Java Beach Café Locations	167

*It is an honor for me to dedicate
this book in memory of*

KJM 7

AMDG

Introduction

I first met Pat Maguire in the middle of the Covid pandemic. It was 2020, a time when the entire world seemed to be upside down. I had come to San Francisco from New Orleans to host a shamanic plant medicine retreat up north. My best friend had recently passed from a rare cancer, and to put it plainly, I was in a full blown existential crisis.

I was staying temporarily in the Mission District, trying to make sense of life, grief, and the strange energy of those uncertain times. On one particular day, I decided to take the N-Judah train out to Cole Valley. There's a little place there called *The Sword and the Rose*, a small, mystical shop. I was hoping to find a rose quartz in remembrance of my friend, ideally one shaped like a heart. When I arrived, the shop was closed. Of course it was. Another disappointment layered onto everything else.

Feeling melancholy, I hopped back on the N-Judah and rode it all the way to the beach. I had read a *New York Times* article that mentioned a café out there with the best avocado toast in town. As a vegan, that had naturally caught my attention. But when I got off at the very last stop, I didn't see the place from the article. Instead, I saw *Java Beach Café*.

"What is this place?" I wondered…

Two guys were outside, loading up their trucks with boxes of food. They were casually juggling a soccer ball back and forth, easily over fifty touches between them before the ball hit the ground. The older one finally said to the younger, "Okay, you're set to go. You do the Tenderloin. I'll do the Bayview. And remember what we were talking about from Corinthians 13… AMDG, KJM7."

"Okay, Paddy," the younger man replied.

"Good man, Paddy," the older one answered.

I thought it was funny both calling each other Paddy. I approached the older man and asked if they served avocado toast. He smiled and said, "We have avocado, and we have toast. We can definitely make that for you."

When my order was ready, the older man called my name through the pickup window they were using during Covid protocols. What struck me immediately was that he pronounced my name correctly. Caeli, pronounced "Chaylee." No barista ever gets that right. Ever. He handed me my drink and my toast with avocado.

Then, almost as if his eyes could see right through the surface, he quickly noticed my tattoo: a rose and a cross, faint and hard to see on my dark skin. He also caught my ankh necklace from Egypt. Without missing a beat, he began talking about a museum in San José that housed Egyptian artifacts, one of the exact reasons I had come to San Francisco in the first place. He mentioned a friend who had passed away, Hughie, who used to wear ankh earrings. Then he went right into stories about how he used to sell Christmas trees across the street, back when it was an empty lot before it became La Playa Park.

From there, the floodgates opened.

Pat talked about the time he visited the pyramids in Egypt, and the strange spiritual phenomena that followed. He told me about the neighborhood's original name, *Carville*, and how his mother had cared for its last surviving resident named Mirdi. They were mystics and bohemians who once lived here in old trolley cars. He told me how he had been hanging out on this corner since he was 15 years old. He described a tunnel that used to run under the Great Highway to the beach, which was torn out in 1989. He spoke about a homeless gang called The Animals who listened to country music, most of whom had died except one man named Big Red who eventually got sober and was the only survivor. He told me about the indigenous people of the Ohlone tribe who once lived in the area. It was like listening to a walking encyclopedia of San Francisco's forgotten past.

"Hey Pat, your truck is ready!" someone called from inside the kitchen.

He turned back to me and said, "Okay, I need to go."

As he was about to leave, he reached into his pocket and handed me a small gift. A rose quartz heart.

I was stunned. I hadn't even told him why I had originally come to the neighborhood. Yet here he was, handing me the exact symbol I was searching for.

In our conversation, I discovered that Pat had once been deeply involved in his church, but as he described it, he had experienced "ontological shock." He said he suffered a horrible tragedy in 2013. Then the chapel where he once brought his children to pray had closed its doors on them during the pandemic, labeling worship as "non-essential." Pat said, "I thought church was most essential, especially in times like this."

I asked him about the Scripture he quoted to young Paddy – Corinthians 13, and about the cryptic AMDG and KJM7. He explained that AMDG was Latin: *Ad Majorem Dei Gloriam*, which translates to "For the greater glory of God." I asked if he spoke Latin. He told me he speaks some Italian and knows a bit of Latin, but if he started explaining KJM7, "we'd be here all day."

We became instant friends. I ended up getting a job offer here in The City, so it became my new home.

Whenever I came back to the beach, I'd head straight for *Java Beach Café*. Over time, I got to know Pat more deeply. I found out that he had a story for everything, and I mean everything. Some are hard to believe. In fact, if he hadn't pulled out that rose quartz heart from his pocket like a Vegas magician, and later explained why he even had it, I may not have believed half of his tales. I told him more than once that he needed to write a book, or else all those stories would be lost forever. He would usually smile and say, "I'll try."

Five years passed, and my friendship with Pat only grew deeper. One day, I overheard him talking with two other men, Kevin and young Paddy, both of whom had written books. Pat said he had finished his memoir "to the best of his ability," but wasn't sure if he wanted to publish it.

He glanced at Kevin's jacket, which had AMDG embroidered on it. "There's another sign," he said calmly, as if the universe was winking at him yet again.

Later that day, I asked him when he planned to publish the story. He said confidently that he wasn't going to publish it. I asked why. He explained that it felt too personal, too sacred, that perhaps it was just something he needed to write for cathartic reasons. I told him that if he didn't publish it, I would write a book about him myself.

Apparently, he took my threat seriously. With a mischievous smile, he handed me his notebook.

"You're giving me your story?" I asked.

"Yes, but only the PG version. The other version was left in a confessional room in Northern Ireland. Some church lady probably found it and was clutching her beads while reading it." He broke out into laughter like a comedian who just nailed his own punchline.

I told him I was heading back to New Orleans to care for my sick mother. But I promised him I would read his story and write an introduction. Pat writes in "dot dot dot" style, and I encouraged him to keep it that way.

He said if the book makes any money he would like to donate a portion to the *Ronald McDonald House*, so families without resources could stay with their sick children during hospital treatments.

I emphatically agreed. I came to this neighborhood for avocado toast and ended up finding its soul. As someone who studies spirituality and mysticism, I feel like I have struck gold.

AMDG & KJM7.

Here is Pat's story.

1

Sunset District Irish

Pat was born into a little shack on Miramar Street, right off Ocean Avenue… Ingleside days… a tight, humble home with a young mother and father and three children…John Joe, Mary, and Pat…

The house couldn't hold the growing family much longer… so they moved… west… toward the wind and sea, out to the Lower Sunset… it was part of a quiet migration… Irish families leaving the Mission District and Ingleside for a new kind of frontier by the beach…

Pat's mother was a native San Franciscan …ICBM, they called it… Irish Catholic Born in the Mission…

His father had crossed the sea from Belfast… chasing the promise of something better… he worked at *Southern Pacific Railroad* down on the Embarcadero… his mother worked at the Main Library downtown, surrounded by stories and silence…

The Sunset became home… Holy Name Parish…and the siblings kept coming… Daniel, Christianne, Thomas, Stephen… a true Irish brood…

It was a different kind of San Francisco then… immigrant families packed into pastel homes with kids tumbling out of every doorway… money was tight, but homes were bought, tuition was paid, and even vacations up to the Russian River weren't impossible dreams…

On 48th and Kirkham stood the San Francisco Ice Arena where he'd skate… out at the beach…Playland… five-and-dimes with red licorice and comic books… bakeries with fresh rolls… supermarkets with butchers who knew your name…

Pat and the neighborhood kids rode their bikes all through Golden Gate Park... so few cars back then, they'd play football in the middle of the street... and when a car did drive through, it waited... the play had to finish...

They grew up on Irish rebel music and American country... the hearth was sacred... Pat's parents were storytellers and the fire was their stage...

The bunk beds creaked as the kids climbed in for the night... all of them packed into that little room... in those days ... barely any TV... just the hum of the old radio in the corner...

Outside... the San Francisco foghorns moaned through the night air... teenagers raced down the Great Highway... their engines screaming into the darkness...

But inside... inside was different... Pat's father would light up a Pall Mall Red... lean back in his bed ... and with the smoke curling toward the ceiling... his voice would carry them away... stories of Ireland... of leprechauns hiding behind mossy stones... of ghosts wandering lonely cliffs... but for Pat... his favorite was always the banshees on Cave Hill...

Pat was always the one who asked why the banshees were crying... his brothers and sisters would groan... "Just let Dad tell the story,"... but Pat couldn't help it... his father would smile... take a long drag... and say... "The banshee is a harbinger for the royal Irish families..." Pat would sit up... "What's a harbinger?... Are we royal?"

His father would pause... the smoke hanging between them like a veil... "We still have a castle in Fermanagh"... but he never answered what a harbinger was... or why the banshees cried... Pat always wondered if his father wasn't telling him something... maybe for a reason... so he would lay back... his hyperphantasiac mind slipping easily into those ancient hills... into the myths... into the trance... into delta waves... where the stories became real... where peace found him... and carried him off to sleep...

Church was something to look forward to... lighting candles, whispering prayers, kneeling beside his parents... Pat prayed to score goals in soccer... Once, before the championship game against the Sons of Italy at Crocker Amazon... he whispered a prayer for a hat trick... the following Monday, his paper route carried his own story... *"Hat Trick Patrick and the Celtics Beat Sons of Italy in Championship, 3–1."*

The world shimmered with magic back then... but the shimmer started to fade in the late '70s... Playland shut down... empty storefronts ... and in their place came cheaply built, lifeless boxes... and gangs... little ones at first... but dangerous just the same...

Pat was a timid boy... small, shy... but he loved the playground at Francis Scott Key... basketball, football, strikeout, roller hockey, softball, tag... capture the flag... up and down Sunset Boulevard until the streetlights blinked on... He had his crew ... like the little rascals ... Fitz, Murph, Callahan, Paulie, Mikey, Mary and Kim... his little brothers, sister Christianne and cousins...all sorts of neighborhood kids...

He also had protectors... his older brother John Joe... his cousin Jimmy ... Golden Gloves fighter... when the gangs came for him, they didn't get far...

Once, cornered at Polly Ann's Ice Cream on Noriega Street by older kids who wanted to beat him up... Pat shook with terror... but someone ran to Holy Name and found John Joe... the thugs scattered like windblown trash when John Joe came flying...

Pat laughed watching them run... but the laugh turned to silence when John Joe turned to him and said... "Pat,... you need to be tough in this world. You need to learn how to fight."

It scared him... but he knew his brother was right... so they built a boxing ring in the backyard... weights... heavy bags... looked more like a prison yard than a play space... Jimmy trained them all... they fought every day...

Judah Street, once lined with warm bakeries and little shops, became something else... bars and liquor stores... Dicks at the Beach... Finian's Rainbow... The Sea Gull... The Reef... Markell's gun store... 7-Eleven on 46th... but through all of it... Pat clung to family, sports... and God...

He had no interest in thug life... in fact, when he was young, he wanted to be a priest... school was a struggle...his head was full of stories, daydreams... but he was polite... respectful... they let him stay...

He ended up in a little special class in the convent with five other kids... he didn't mind... Mikey was there, too... and there was Sister Rose Marie... a nun who saw something in Pat... she taught him a prayer called the *Memorare*... told him if he prayed it with his whole heart, it would never fail... he believed her... because even then... the world already felt like a battle... and Pat knew he'd need all the help he could get...

2

Bye, Dad

When Pat was fifteen years old… his father was dying of cancer… One night… as his father neared the last weeks of life… he called Pat to his bedside… "Pat… I'm going to ask you something… I need you to promise me… never drink alcohol or do drugs."…what he may not have known… Pat had already been drinking since he was thirteen… but how could he not honor the dying request of the man he loved most in this world?…

"Okay, Dad… I will do that…"

Pat's father died on October 21st, 1982… the night he passed, his family was gathered in the hospital room… his father told them his two old friends, Joe and Neil, were in the room… they'd died years before… but he saw them… standing there… waiting for him… Pat was the last one to leave his hospital room… he wouldn't go… not until his father looked at him… not until he said goodbye…

His dad was slipping in and out of consciousness… but finally… he turned his head… "Goodbye, Pat…" Pat wanted so badly to say *I love you*… but the words stuck… all he could say was… "Goodbye…"

And then he ran… his mother… his six brothers and sisters… were walking toward the elevator… Pat chased after them, yelling … "He woke up! He said goodbye to me!" he didn't know if they believed him… but he knew it was true… a few hours later… he was gone…

Ten days later… Halloween night… Pat's friends were up at Francis Scott Key schoolyard… drinking beer… he told them he couldn't go… he had to honor his father… but then… his little brother Thomas came flying up on a bike… "Pat! Get up to the schoolyard! There's a gang up there … chains, bats, everything! They're gonna start a fight!"

There were twenty of them… only eight of Pat's friends… he ran… when he got there, a huge kid was screaming …

"Who wants to fight?"… wild… frothing at the mouth… he punched Pat's cousin in the face… his cousin … gentle, not a fighter …ran away, blood pouring from his nose… Pat confronted them… "Hey! Fight me!"

The big kid turned, amused… Pat was small… but he stood in front of him… they squared off on the basketball courts at the Key… the first punch… lights… Pat hit the ground…

"Get up, you little pussy!"

One eye swelled shut… he got up, shaking… terrified… the second punch landed harder… more lights… Pat went down again… flat on his back… the kid stood over him, beating his chest… his crew laughed…

Pat looked around… saw the faces of his brothers, his friends… fear everywhere… the kid was picking out his next target… and something inside Pat decided … he would rather die than let them be hurt… he got up…

"I'm not done!"

The kid turned, surprised… charged at Pat… Pat ducked… threw a left hook… the kid dropped… flat on his knees… he scrambled up… Pat threw a right… down again… silence…

His crew froze… weapons in their hands… Pat should've finished him… kicked him in the face… ended it… but something in him paused… instead, he stood over him… beat his chest… "Get up, you pussy!"

Pat started circling the gang … "Who's next?"… they looked at each other… confused… afraid… behind Pat, the kid started rising again…

"Let's go! I can go all night!" Pat said … Pat started bouncing… moving like his cousin taught him… his boxing coach… but then… the kid held up a hand … "Hey… I'm done… I can't do this anymore…"

Pat didn't trust him… but the kid was serious… he reached out his hand … "Hey, man… I respect you…"

Pat wanted to hit him again… but he could barely see through his swollen eyes… he hesitated… then slowly… shook the kid's hand…

"What's your name?" the kid asked. "You're the toughest kid I ever fought…"

"My name is Pat Maguire… and this is my schoolyard… these are my people."… Pat pointed to his family… his friends… "If you ever come here again and disrespect them… I'm coming after you…"

The kid nodded… "I hear you…"

His crew left… heads down… weapons unused… and Pat… walked home down Kirkham Street… something had changed in him… he had always been scared… even though he could fight… he had always been scared… but now… he wasn't…

He looked at his friend Mikey… "Give me a beer…"

"You sure, Mac?"

"Yeah… give me one."… Mikey handed him a Budweiser… Pat chugged it down… and thought… *I'm sorry, Dad*… but this world is tough… and I need to be tougher…

He broke his promise… but he had people to protect now… and he had people to hunt… people who had wronged him were going to pay… he was going to protect his family… his friends… his neighborhood… he was going to unleash hell on this earth… and only death would stop him…

He went home… put ice on his face… laid on the couch… whispered into the dark… "I'm sorry, Dad…"

3

Revenge List

Pat returned to school a week after the fight with the big kid… both his eyes were swollen shut… not exactly the look St. Ignatius wanted from a sophomore… he kept quiet… said nothing when people asked what happened… just shrugged…

But back in the neighborhood… word was already spreading… a kid approached him with a smirk… "They're saying you lost… the guy's friends are telling everyone…"

Something shifted inside Pat… the fear was gone… vengeance had taken its place… "Where does that kid hang out?" Pat asked…

"Your Market… 48th Avenue… plays pinball there…"

Pat turned to his younger brother Daniel… only thirteen… but already a Golden Gloves fighter… "Let's go," Pat said… "I need backup…"

They walked down to Your Market… and there he was… Pat tapped him on the shoulder… the kid turned… his eyes wide… "Let's go outside… we gotta fight…"

The kid blinked… "Why? I thought we were cool…"

"I thought so too… but your boys are out there running their mouths… saying I lost… so let's settle it…" but the wild guy from the schoolyard was gone… and so was the scared kid Pat used to be… they had switched places… the kid looked terrified now…

"I don't want to fight you," he said… "I never want to fight you again…"

Pat didn't care… "You need to… because I need to shut your boys up…"

"They're not even my friends," the kid said …"I'll tell them I didn't win…"

"Give me their names," Pat demanded… he did… five names…

That's where it started… the list… the vengeance list…

It didn't stop there… Pat wasn't just after him anymore… he wanted all of them… the bullies from Polly Ann's Ice Cream Shop… the ones who stole his basketball at the schoolyard… the guys who jumped him on the way to soccer practice at Beach Chalet… the punks who took his money at the Riordan basketball game… the ones who chased him and his brothers down Judah Street…

Every face that ever tried to break him… he made a list… and one by one… he hunted them down… He trained every day… his fists sharp… his rage sharper…

His mother worked nights at Laguna Honda Hospital… and their house slowly turned into something like *The Outsiders*… kids with nowhere to go started showing up… the first was Pat Lawlor… then two Irish twins from Ballymun… a kid from Gweedore… three guys named Dennis — one they called Chico…

And as the years went on… more came… kids from the neighborhood… the O'Boyle's, Naughton's, Cotters, Currans, Hackett, Fitz, kids from the Excelsior… Philpott… Hatzis … Matias… the Ford brothers…all the youngsters …his little brothers and friends…the cousins… the McKenzie's and Keith's…the Sunset Irish stronghold was born… they protected each other… but the list remained… Pat found them at keggers in Golden Gate Park… at Ocean Beach… Stern Grove… West Sunset… they didn't know him… but he knew them… and one by one… he got them all…

When he found the guys from Polly Ann's… he never told them who he was… He'd bump into them and say… "Hey… watch where you're walking."… then the fists would fly… and every time he hit… he thought about that day… standing there with mint chocolate chip dripping down his hand… shaking as they threatened him… and he hit harder…

Eventually, he didn't just fight for himself anymore… he started fighting for others… the bully hunter of the Sunset… weekdays were for training… weekends were for alcohol and violence… and it went on like that… for years…

But there was one name he couldn't cross off… the leader of the West

Sunset gang… eight years older… harder to find… Pat believed that if he could get him… then maybe… finally… he'd find peace…

One afternoon… walking up Lawton Street… hunting for some people who crossed him… weapon in his pocket… ready to do real damage… he passed the church… the doors were open… it wasn't Sunday… it was Wednesday… *Why was it open?*… He didn't know… but his feet carried him inside…

He knelt in the pew… the rage still swirling inside… then he heard a voice… a priest from Africa… a missions appeal Mass… the words cut through the storm… "Jesus Christ… Son of the living God… have mercy on me, a sinner…"

Pat whispered it… then again… and again… and then… it happened… his body started shaking… tears poured… the room spun… a light approached him… or maybe he approached the light… he couldn't tell…

His entire life played out before him… every fight… every wound… every moment of fear… and then… he and the light merged… he felt love… pure… complete… He felt forgiven… free… at peace…

Pat stood up and walked out of that church a different man… At home… he grabbed a Bible… flipped through its pages… and there it was… staring back at him like a fist to the face… *"You hypocrite… you try to take the speck out of another's eye… while a log sits in your own… first, tend to yourself…"* He knew it was true…

That was the day he stopped drinking… the day he decided to change his life… he went around the neighborhood… trying to make peace… telling everyone… "I met Jesus…" He thought they'd be happy for him… but behind his back… he heard the whispers… "Did you hear?… Pat's gone crazy… he's lost his mind"… they didn't understand… but he didn't care…

The revenge tour was over… now it was a redemption tour… and the road was only just beginning…

4

Carville and the Coffee House

When Pat was a kid… people called him a daydreamer… teachers said he didn't pay attention… and maybe he didn't… he'd go so deep into his thoughts… so deep he couldn't hear the world around him…

Later in life… he'd learn there was a name for that state… theta brain waves… the space between waking and dreaming… where the spirit world feels closer…

In 1991… Pat had one of those moments that would never leave him… He was sitting on the stairs next to the bathroom on Judah Street… a 7-Eleven coffee in his hand… He drifted into that deep, dreamy space… his imagination …or what he thought was imagination…took over… he started daydreaming of Carville…

Carville… that old commune of bohemians and mystics who lived in abandoned railway cars by the ocean… it wasn't just a legend to Pat… when he was a boy, his mother cared for the last living resident of Carville… a blind woman… 103 years old… She told stories about the neighborhood… Judah and La Playa had been their world… ground zero for the mystics… Now here he was… sitting on Judah Street… near that same sacred ground… thinking about people like the great Colonel Daly who once walked it…

Pat looked across the street… saw the old boarded up bar… Dick's at the Beach… It had been shut down since the 1989 Loma Prieta earthquake… the one that struck during the World Series between the Giants and the A's… a section of the Bay Bridge collapsed that day… Pat had just driven over the spot where it gave way… He never forgot that moment… a narrow escape that stayed etched in his body…

Then a thought came…uninvited but clear… "Open a coffee house there."

Pat blinked… confused… *How am I supposed to know how to do that?* he asked himself… but in that dreamlike state… something stirred… he could hear the sounds of Playland at the Beach… laughter… roller coasters… the clang of carnival rides… Laughing Sal's eerie cackle echoing in his mind… the smell of ocean air… popcorn… hot dogs…

And then… another thought… or maybe a calling… *Rebuild this neighborhood.* Pat shook his head… *But how?* No answer… just a deep, still knowing…

He stood up… walked across the street… peered through a crack in the boarded up window… the interior was dark… dust clung to every surface… It had been abandoned for years… There was a faded "For Rent" sign… it had been there for half a decade…

Nobody wanted the place… most of Judah Street was a ghost town… what remained was scattered… the Reef bar on 48th Avenue… Markell's gun store… 7-Eleven on 46th… a few liquor stores… a halfway house for recovering addicts… Celia's Mexican restaurant… Other Avenues – the hippie co-op… but everything else was gone…

The loss that hit Pat hardest was the ice rink on 48th… that place had saved kids like him… a second home in the lower Sunset District… he and his friends had spent days and nights there…

He stared into the dark… hollow shell of the bar… and then… a vision… not a thought… not a hope… but a crystal clear image… a coffee house… alive with energy… a gathering place… a rebirth… He saw shops open again… people laughing… community forming… the neighborhood pulsing with new life…

He thought to himself… *Okay… let's do this.*

The vision remained… unwavering… and Pat walked home… that day never left him… it wasn't just imagination… it was something more… something sacred…

5

The Promise (If I Saw You in Heaven)

February 4th... 1992... it was a cold, gray morning... Pat was riding with his friend Mike... on their way to work... They worked in Oakland... for a company called Service West... they installed office furniture in all the high-rise buildings... the crew they worked with was... well... eclectic to say the least...

There were Vietnam veterans... ex-convicts... hippies... wanderers... even survivors of Jonestown... including some of Jim Jones' children... and then there was a whole crew of Sunset District kids... Pat was responsible for hiring most of those kids... He'd go down to the beach at Kelly's Cove... "Hey! Who needs a job?"... Whoever raised their hand... he'd say... "Alright... let's go."

He ran the night crew... unloading trucks filled with office furniture... Then he'd be back in the morning for the installation of cubicles... He worked 12 to 16 hours a day... every day... But that morning was different...

It was a sad day... their good friend Tom Landers had just fallen 40 feet while working at the new sewer plant... He was in a coma at General Hospital... Tom was more than a friend... he and Pat had worked side construction jobs together... they'd laugh and dream about things...

Pat used to tell Tom about his dream of opening a coffee house someday... Tom thought it was hilarious... "You mean like one of those hippie places in North Beach?" he'd ask... He'd belly laugh as he said it...

"Yes! Exactly like that!" Pat would tell him... Pat wasn't exactly the coffee house type back then... but after his spiritual awakening at 22... he had stopped drinking alcohol for a time... and coffee houses became a refuge for him... He'd ask Tom if he wanted to help him build it someday... Tom would laugh even harder... "Sure... why not?"... It became a running joke between them...

As Pat and Mike drove that morning... talking about Tom... a sudden feeling came over Pat... it wasn't just a thought... it was something deeper... He turned to Mike and said... "Let's go say goodbye to Tom... he's about to die."

Mike didn't hesitate... he immediately turned the truck around... and they headed to San Francisco General Hospital... When they arrived... they saw Tom's mother in the waiting area... she had been there all night... she was exhausted... she needed to go home and rest...

They asked if they could see Tom... she nodded and said, "Go ahead..." They walked into Tom's room... he was lying there... motionless... machines surrounding him... the rhythmic beeping filled the room... then... the flatline sound echoed...

Pat ran out of the room... desperate to find help... Just then... he saw a Catholic priest walking down the hall... "Father... please help... my friend is dying," he said... Without a word... the priest followed him into the room... he began administering last rites... Pat held Tom's hand... when he took his final breaths... Pat leaned down... and whispered to him... "I'm going to open that coffee house... I promise."

Those were the last words Pat spoke to him... before he departed... Pat and Mike walked out in silence... they got back in the truck... and started driving to work...

That's when the radio came on... A song began to play... They had never heard it before... The words sent a chill down Pat's spine... *"Would it be the same... if I saw you in heaven?"*

It was a song written by Eric Clapton... about losing his child... Pat and Mike looked at each other... They didn't say anything at first... finally... Pat broke the silence... "Okay... now I really need to open that coffee house."

Mike nodded... "I'll do it with you too... if you want."

The air felt heavy... but something shifted inside Pat... He had made a promise... and he intended to keep it...

6

The Deal

After Pat made the promise to Tom… he knew he had to try… he had to go through the steps of opening a coffee house… at the time… he still thought of it as his wild imagination… the spirits of Carville guiding him… but now… he believed he had Tom with him as well…

He called the number on the "For Rent" sign outside the old bar on Judah Street… the sign had been hanging there for five years… a kind and gentle man answered… "Mr. Lee,…" Pat explained that he wanted to open a coffee house in the building… Mr. Lee didn't hesitate… "Come over," he said… "Let's discuss it." They set a date and time…

That's when it hit Pat… he didn't look or dress like a business owner… all he had were construction clothes… hoodies… Ben Davis pants… and a closet full of 49ers ball caps… so… he went to Ross Dress for Less… he bought what he thought was business attire… a collared shirt… Dockers… and a briefcase… he didn't have a clue what should go inside the briefcase… but he bought it anyway…

The day of the meeting… he walked from his mother's house down Judah Street… he stood in front of the door at 1396 La Playa… staring at the doorbell… he reached his finger toward it… and suddenly… fear overwhelmed him…

You must be insane, he thought… *You can't do this!* He turned away… took three steps toward home… but then… something stopped him… it wasn't just a thought… it was a force… he turned back around… walked to the door… and rang the bell… Mr. Lee opened the door…

Pat stood there… feeling foolish… wearing his new shirt and pants… holding a briefcase with nothing inside… not even a pen or paper… completely empty… like his wallet… and his bank account… a handful of nothing… Mr. Lee smiled warmly… he invited Pat upstairs…

"Wow… you're quite young… How old are you?" he asked…

"I'm 25 years old, sir," Pat replied…

He raised an eyebrow… "And you want to open a coffee shop? Like a restaurant?"

"No," Pat said quickly… "It's not like a restaurant… it's more like a European coffee house… like the ones in North Beach… the kind of place where the hippies used to hang out."

Mr. Lee nodded thoughtfully… In the 1990s… coffee houses had become rare in San Francisco… Their heyday had been in the 1960s…

Mr. Lee's eyes lit up… "That's an incredible idea," he said… "It could be something special." He then told Pat that he had been planning to get rid of the commercial space altogether… He was going to pull permits next week to turn the bar into a living unit… but he said he loved Pat's vision… and he wanted to give him a chance…

They shook hands… "I'll give you a year of free rent to build the place," Mr. Lee said… "It's in bad shape… You'll need the time."

Pat thanked him… and explained that he worked 16-hour days in construction… installing office spaces… Mr. Lee nodded… understanding…

Pat walked home with so much to think about… When he opened the door to his mother's house… he announced… "Mom… I made the deal!" She looked at him like he had just killed the cat… her face was a mix of disbelief and shock… not the excitement he had hoped for…

"How do you plan on doing this?" she asked…

He grinned… "Don't worry, Mom… I got this!"… but deep inside… he didn't have a clue… and he knew it…

7

At Least I Tried

After making the deal with Mr. Lee… Pat had a plan… His brother John Joe and his best friend Mikey would construct the café… while Pat figured out the coffee business… Since Pat was just a modular furniture installer… he didn't have the skills to build the café himself… and when it came to coffee… all he knew was how to make a cup of Folgers instant at home… But life had other plans…

Just as they were getting ready to start construction… a hurricane hit Hawaii… it destroyed the islands… and they needed construction workers from all over the country to help rebuild… the offer was too good to pass up… Free room and board… excellent pay… John Joe and Mikey left for Hawaii…

So that left Pat… alone… trying to figure out how to pull this off… he knew he was in way over his head… then he remembered his co-worker and friend, Mike… Mike had said he'd help if needed… so… they got to work… doing whatever they could to build the place…

While they worked… they started investigating the world of coffee… there was a place in the South of Market called Capricorn Coffee… they made the best cup Pat had ever tasted… the foreman on the day crew at Service West…Larry…always had a thermos of it… whenever he wasn't looking… Pat would sneak a cup for himself…

He reached out to Capricorn Coffee… that's when he met Angelina… she was one of their salespeople… and as it turned out… a good friend of

Mikey's older brother Bernie… Angelina was happy to help… She offered to teach them the coffee business…

They were finally making progress… but it wasn't easy… the stress was overwhelming… In a moment of weakness… Pat decided to have a beer… he'd been sober for a while… ever since his spiritual awakening years earlier… he thought… "A couple beers won't hurt."… Boy… was he wrong… The dream started to unravel… slowly… but surely… until it came to a complete halt…

One rainy day… Pat found himself sitting in a trench at the old bar… staring at a hopeless plumbing situation… the pipes were broken… rusted… he felt defeated… *What am I doing?* he thought… *I'm just a crazy fool…* he decided right then and there… to give up…

Maybe I should just stick to what I know… install office cubicles… buy a house in Concord… with a swimming pool… find a wife… have ten kids… live happily ever after… He even thought about the Sunset District lottery… those lucky few who landed stable city jobs… They were the successful ones…

He stood up… soaked from the rain… he locked the door to 1396 La Playa… he started mentally preparing himself for the conversation he'd have with Mr. Lee… he'd have to tell him he couldn't finish what he had started… Pat walked home in the rain…

When he got home… he collapsed onto his mother's living room couch… the same couch that served as his bed… he fell asleep almost instantly…

A few hours later… he woke up to the sound of the TV… It was still on… a movie was playing… *One Flew Over the Cuckoo's Nest,* starring Jack Nicholson… he sat up… groggy… just in time to catch a scene that would change everything…

Nicholson's character was standing in the room with the other patients… he pointed to the massive sink and declared… "I'm going to pick up that sink and throw it through the window!"… the other patients laughed at him… he struggled to lift it… veins bulging… straining with everything he had… but the sink wouldn't budge… the laughter grew louder…

Then… Nicholson glared at them and said… "At least I tried… you goddamn morons!"… It wasn't the most polite line… but in that moment…

something in Pat clicked… a light bulb went on… He stood up… put on his shoes…

"That's it!" he said out loud… "I'll at least try!" He wasn't going to quit… he was going to metaphorically throw the sink through the window… he was going to build that coffee house…

8

The First Customer

With a new sense of determination… Pat marched back down to Judah Street… it was still raining… but it didn't matter… *At least I'll try*, he said to himself…

He unlocked the door to 1396 La Playa… stepped inside… and began concocting a plan… he stood there… near the entrance… trying to map out what needed to be done… that's when he noticed a little guy walking toward him… the man had an aura about him… almost like a leprechaun… he couldn't have been more than 5'5"… and he had two little dogs with him… Pat sighed inwardly… He didn't really want to talk to him… every time someone stopped by and asked what he was doing… the conversation was always the same…

"What are you building?" they'd ask…

"A coffee house," he'd reply…

And 100 percent of the time… the response was discouraging… "I don't see that working down here." Pat hated hearing it… it annoyed him to no end… *Well… I didn't ask for your opinion*, he'd think… so when this little guy approached and asked… "What are you building?"… Pat was tempted to tell him to kick rocks… but something stopped him… this time… he didn't brush him off…

"I'm building a coffee house," he said…

He braced himself for the usual response… expecting the man to ask… "Like a restaurant?"… then he'd have to go through the whole explanation again… but he didn't… instead… the man paused for a moment... and said... "You mean like a coffee house from the 1960s? With poetry... and open mics?"

Pat lit up... "Yes! Exactly!"

The man stood still... closed his eyes... and took a deep breath... then... silence... an uncomfortable, awkward silence... he didn't move or say a word... for what felt like an hour... even though it was probably just a minute... finally... he spoke...

"I'm a psychic," he said... "This place is going to be highly successful... It's going to change this neighborhood forever."

In the past... Pat probably would have brushed off someone like him... dismissed him as some kook... but in that moment... he didn't... he nodded... and said sincerely... "Thank you, sir. What's your name?" he asked...

The man smiled... "Angelo," he said... "and I'm going to be your first customer when you open." Pat stood there... watching Angelo walk away with his two little dogs... For the first time in a long while... he felt something he hadn't felt before... Hope...

9

Miracles & Machines

Pat felt so much better now… someone finally believed in his project… even if it was just an odd stranger claiming to be a psychic… but deep down… he knew the truth… yes… he knew… he must at least try…

He went inside the café and started cleaning… the place was a disaster… he rolled up his sleeves and got to work…

About an hour later… he noticed someone peering through the window… it was Mike Roddy… his old high school rugby coach… Mike owned a bar up on Noriega called Roddy's Fish Bowl… he had a reputation… he'd kicked Pat out of that place before for barroom brawling… they had a love-hate relationship… Mike said whatever was on his mind… didn't care if he offended you… he was a big… tough guy… who could handle himself in a fight… but man… was he hilarious… his blunt truth and humor often got him into scraps… but Pat couldn't help but admire the guy…

Mike walked in and said… "I heard you're trying to open a coffee house… How's that going?"

Pat sighed… "Not well… John Joe and Mikey went to Hawaii… I don't have money… or the know-how to build this place… I started drinking again… Everyone thinks I'm crazy… and maybe they're right…"

Mike laughed… "What do you need done?"

Pat shook his head… "Everything… plumbing… electrical… sheetrock… paint… wainscoting… tile… ceilings… bathrooms… kitchen… appliances…"

Mike just laughed harder… "Maybe I can help," he said…

Pat was stunned… The last time they'd spoken, Mike was throwing him out of his bar… but now… he was offering to help…

"I've got a bunch of guys sitting in my bar doing nothing 'cause of the rain," Mike said… "I'll bring them tomorrow… but you gotta supply the beer."

"Deal!" Pat said eagerly…

Sure enough… Mike showed up the next day with a crew…all the neighborhood guys… Moylan, Sullivan, Tehan, etc … they worked just for beer… for three weeks straight… the café was nearly finished…more troops arrived…Thorson, Wells, McPolin, Scott … plumbing… electrical… walls… all done…the Collins brothers built the bar and cabinets… all that was left was the ceiling… the paint… and the appliances…

Mike said… "I'll see if Doug can help with the painting."

Doug showed up with their friend Frank… they started painting right away… while they worked… Doug looked up at the ceiling… it was a beautiful wooden ceiling from the early 1900s…

"What are you planning to do with that?" he asked…

"Probably tear it out and put in acoustic tiles… It's cheaper," Pat said…

Doug shook his head… "Don't do that… this is a special ceiling… I'll restore it… don't worry about the money."

Frank looked at him like he'd lost his mind… but bless his heart… he stayed to help… with Doug and Frank busy on the ceiling… Pat focused on equipment… he figured he'd need about $50,000… he planned to earn it by working long hours at Service West…

Pat went to a restaurant supply store with a list of everything he needed… the salesperson was friendly… "I love your enthusiasm," the man said… "I'll get you a great deal."… Pat felt hopeful… until he saw the price… "I can get you everything for $150,000!" the guy said… Pat's heart sank…

On the way home… he stopped for a beer to clear his head… Bad idea… he didn't return to the job site for three days… he was exhausted… ashamed… when he finally showed up… Doug and Frank were still working… they weren't mad… but they were concerned…

"Where've you been?" they asked…

Pat told them the truth… "I got discouraged… I couldn't afford the equipment... so I went for a beer." That's when the first miracle happened...

Frank said... "My brother has all that kind of equipment in storage... from an old café that got torn out... he purchases abandoned units... I'll ask if he'll sell it to you."

The second miracle came when Doug and Frank shared something personal... "We quit drinking, too," they said... "We had a spiritual experience... we belong to a group... if you think you have a problem... we can bring you."

Pat hesitated... terrified... "Maybe I do..." he whispered...

"Great," they said... "We'll take you tonight." Pat's mind raced...

"What's happening to my life?" he thought... That night... Pat found himself in a room full of people talking about God... It wasn't a Catholic setting... which scared him even more...

"I'm Catholic," he told them... "I don't think I can be here..."

They smiled... "Catholics are welcome," they said gently... Pat didn't understand what was happening... but these were the kindest... most nonjudgmental people he'd ever met... and they were sober...

The next day... Frank's brother, Brian, took Pat to the storage unit... It was filled with everything he needed...

Pat asked nervously... "How much for all of it?"

Brian smiled... "You know what... I was about to throw this stuff away... you can have it for $5,000."

Pat couldn't believe it... the café was built... furnished... and ready for business... Angelina began training him on how to make coffee... now he needed workers... he heard about a Sunset girl named Maureen who worked at the coffee shop in Stonestown... he asked how much she made...

"Six dollars an hour," she said...

"I'll give you nine," he offered...

She hesitated... then said softly... "Okay..." He had his first shift leader...

The grand opening was around the corner...

As he walked to another meeting with Doug and Frank... Pat pondered what had just happened... they were talking about a God that wasn't necessarily Catholic... and wasn't necessarily not... he was terrified... but... again... he was filled with hope.

10

Against All Odds

The flyers were out… unfortunately… he wasn't the greatest speller… he spelled espresso wrong… *Expresso*…

Opening day was fast approaching… March 20, 1993… Pat was trying to remember everything… which one was the cappuccino… the latte… the Americano… he couldn't figure out the register… had no idea how to operate the espresso machine… it was chaos… but they had Maureen… Rain… Michelle… Angelina… Mike,… his family – the entire Maguire family… and a few random folks who'd signed up to help open the place… They named it *Java Beach*…

Saturday morning… the crowd outside was growing… panic set in… *What have we gotten ourselves into?* Familiar faces in the crowd… a women's soccer team he used to coach… Sunset neighbors… city workers… curious onlookers… Nobody had seen a crowd like that on Judah Street in decades…

Even The Animals, the local homeless gang were there… they'd been hanging around Judah for years… Pat knew he needed some kind of security… so he struck a deal with Big Red Mike Flare and his crew… bought them a case of vodka and told them to keep troublemakers away… they happily agreed…

He walked to the door… heart pounding… it was time… He grabbed the handle… took a deep breath… opened the door… and there he was…

first in line… just like he said he would be… Angelo… the little psychic… He walked in grinning…

"What did I tell you?" he said… "I knew this place would be a success!"

The line didn't stop that day… or the next day… or the next week… or month… or year… Against all odds… it kept going…

11

Buffy

In those early months... Pat was only 26... the stress was overwhelming... and the way he dealt with stress back then... was through self-medication...

He'd do well for a while... then convince himself he could handle just one beer... he was wrong... every time... those relapses landed him in two halfway houses... two inpatient programs... and two outpatient programs... Eventually... he ended up in Europe... seeking ultimate recovery...

During those first months at Java Beach... he started drinking again... it was a turning point... he ended up at Serenity Knolls... and later... Serenity House... a palatial Victorian in Alamo Square... owned by the Archdiocese of San Francisco... that's where he met Billy... Billy knew about his martial arts background... took him on as a student... trained him well over the next few years...

Back at Java Beach... he was working 17-hour days... a friend told him about a girl coming in for a job...

"Her dad's on a long vacation," the friend said... "He wants to make sure she's taken care of...and trust me... her dad's not the kind of guy you want to upset... so keep an eye on her."

Pat nodded... "No problem. I'll train her."

A convertible Porsche pulled up... a young woman stepped out... their eyes met... time... stopped... it was palpable... like something out of a dream... She walked over... he shook her hand...

"You must be Buffy," he said...

"Yes… I'm here for the job."

"I'm Pat… I'll be training you today."

There was something mystical in the air… Pat felt like he had always known her… it was strange… almost eerie… he tried to focus… stay professional… teach her the coffee… they got started… At one point… he complimented her car…

"Nice car… but I've got one that could outrun yours."

She laughed… "No chance!"

He grinned… "I've got a Mustang 5.0."

She laughed harder…

"No way can you out-race me." Her confidence shook him… so he lied…

"Well… I've got a CHP computer chip in my car… so there!"

She rolled her eyes… laughing again… Buffy told him she was born and raised in San Francisco… just like him… she went to Smith College in Northampton… Pat didn't know what that meant… he didn't hang out with college types…

"Do you want to race cars sometime? Or hang out?" he asked…

She laughed… "Sure."

"How about tonight?"

She seemed surprised… but said… "Okay… sure."

That night… he picked her up in his Mustang… they went to Westlake Joe's… neither of them knew the magnitude of that moment… but something had shifted… something that would change his life forever…

12

The Deep Connection

Meeting Buffy changed everything for Pat… he had sworn off relationships… too much heartbreak… too many ghosts from the past still rattling around his spirit… but Buffy was… different…

She wasn't trying to save him… or fix him… she had her own life… her own rhythm… school… family… purpose… they built a friendship… real… slow… steady…

At the time… Pat had just finished a rehab program in Marin… was living at the Victorian sober house in Alamo Square… training in Kung Fu with Billy… he was working long hours at Java Beach… barely sleeping… barely breathing… and he was deep in a spiritual program Doug and Frank had introduced him to…

One day… they handed him an assignment… "Write an inventory of your life," they said… "Confess it to someone who'll understand… then make peace with everyone you've hurt… or hated… or been hurt by…"

Pat didn't like that plan… *Why can't we just leave the past in the past?* he thought… *Isn't that enough?*

One afternoon… driving around the city… Pat told Buffy about the program… about the strange spiritual assignments… she listened… quietly… without judgment… she didn't flinch… didn't try to fix him… just sat with him in the truth… and that truth became their bond…

Their friendship grew… when she told him she'd be out of town for her birthday weekend…turning twenty …he nodded… wished her a good trip… that weekend… Pat had another assignment… making coffee for the group… but before he got there… a thought whispered in his head… *Maybe I should have just one beer… Just one…*

He walked into The Reef bar… sat down… ordered… one beer turned into two… two turned into too many… that night… he spiraled… alcohol… pills… despair… he woke up in General Hospital… barely alive…

Meanwhile… somewhere out in the world… Buffy was on her birthday trip… Suddenly… she felt it… a wave of dread washed over her…

"Pat's dying," she said aloud to her friends… "I can feel it…"

They brushed it off… told her she was being dramatic… but she knew what she felt… something in her spirit knew before the world did… while she was looking for a way to reach him… he was lying in a hospital bed… unconscious… somehow… across time and space… soul to soul… they were connected… not by logic… not by words… but by something deeper…

Something sacred…

13

The Road to Grace

After the near-death experience... most people assumed it would be the wake-up call Pat needed to get sober... but in truth... it became the turning point in the opposite direction... Pat decided sobriety wasn't going to work... so he chose the spiral... full throttle... until the wheels gave out... he even turned against the spiritual program Doug and Frank had introduced him to... the one that had once offered hope and structure... Pat started calling it a cult...

Buffy was still around... in college mostly... drifting in and out of Pat's orbit... every now and then... when she came back to San Francisco... Pat would try to clean up... but the timing never aligned... she began to see the mess... the slide... and yet... she stayed kind... stayed near... when most others had started to disappear... By then... Pat had become too much for even the most loyal of friends...

One day... Buffy mentioned she needed to drive her car back to North Hampton... without thinking... Pat said, "I want to go."

To his surprise... she said, "Okay... you can come."

At that point... Pat was using every day... alcohol...uppers ...just to function... it had been two years since the hospital... the overdose... the only time he was ever truly sober... was when he slept... sometimes for three days straight...

Before the trip... Pat asked his friend Paulie to score him some Bennies—stimulants that gave him the illusion of stability... he didn't want to show Buffy the worst of it… the mean drunk he became without the meds…

Buffy and Pat were supposed to leave at 9:00 a.m… but Paulie never showed… Pat panicked… he considered canceling… but something… hope, maybe God …pushed him forward…

Maybe I'll find more on the road, he thought… so they left… in her red Toyota 4Runner…

Running on the last of his Bennies… Pat talked nonstop… free-styled raps… joked… he rapped through Nevada… through Arizona… through Texas… until finally… he passed out…

He woke up in Shamrock, Texas… a gas station… morning sun pouring through the windshield… and something was different… there was peace… it felt like grace… Buffy turned toward him and smiled, "Good morning."

Pat blinked… "Oh… hey there."

"You've been asleep for a while."

And that's when it hit him… he had no drugs in his system… first time in years… and… he felt okay…

They got back on the road… Buffy didn't know he had run out… didn't know he was riding clean… After a while, she said… "Hey Pat… can you do me a favor?"

"Sure," he said.

She grinned… "Please… no more rapping."

Pat laughed… "Okay… deal."

They stopped at Graceland… Elvis's home… they walked the halls… saw the jumpsuits… the gold records… but Pat wasn't thinking about Elvis… he was thinking about the quiet inside his body… and the stillness in his mind… they ate at the Graceland Café… burgers… fries… Cokes… something so simple… yet it felt… miraculous…

He looked at her… "Can I tell you something?"

"Of course," she said.

"I think I can live like this someday…"

She tilted her head… "Like what?"

"Like sober… doing normal things… with you."

She stared at him… surprised… "Really? Are you serious?"

"Yes… I'd love to marry you someday… have kids… go to their games… live a normal life."

She blinked… unsure whether to believe it…

"You don't even call me your girlfriend… and now you want to marry me?"

Pat nodded… "Someday… yes."

She paused… then softly said… "Well… you have some things to work on… before that could happen."

"I know," he replied.

What she didn't know… was that for the first time in years… Pat didn't want to die… he wanted to live… and he wanted to live because of her… It didn't last… not in the way they might've hoped… but it did mark something sacred…

That moment in the café… at Graceland… where Pat tasted what life could be… a glimpse of a future… a road to grace…

14

The Fall

That moment of grace at Graceland… was short-lived… but… in a strange way… it has lasted a lifetime…

When Buffy and Pat arrived in Boston… she seemed hopeful… hopeful that what they shared in Graceland meant something real… she hadn't seen him clean since the early days of Serenity House… back when Pat was still trying to climb out of the wreckage… it was Pat's birthday while they were there… and Buffy bought them tickets to see the Bruins play the Rangers…

Pat was excited… he'd been a Bruins fan since his childhood… back when he used to skate at the rink on 48th and Kirkham… but then… the cracks began to show…

Buffy had class that day… Pat was left alone at her place… Sobriety… though just two days in…started to feel… uncomfortable… the itch… the gnawing voice… started whispering… "Just one drink… just take the edge off…"

He headed into town… told himself it was just for a beer… he found a small bar… ordered a Heineken… then another… then another… three in… and the whisper turned into a demand… *You need something stronger.*

Pat wandered into a part of Northampton that reminded him of Haight Street… grunge kids… goth kids… lurking like ghosts… he asked if anyone had Bennies…

"Nah," one of them said… "We got weed… and heroin…"

Heroin… the line he'd never crossed…

"Okay," Pat said. "Just give me some weed."

On his way back to Buffy's… he stopped to buy a 12-pack of Olympia… drank the whole thing… smoked all the weed… by the time Buffy got home from class… he was a mess… her face fell… excitement replaced by sadness… but still… they went to the game…

By the time they got to Boston… Pat was belligerent… hostile… she thought about leaving him there… but she knew what that could mean… knew how dangerous that might be… she drove him back to her place… he passed out…

In the morning… Buffy was waiting…

"You need to go," she said calmly… firmly…

Pat didn't argue… he needed to get back to San Francisco anyway… back to what he knew… and he believed the same thing he always believed in moments like this… *I'm just a problem… she's better off without me…*

She drove him to the airport… drove off without even saying goodbye… Pat was sure she was done… when he got back to San Francisco… he dove headfirst into a bender… three weeks of blackout chaos…

Somewhere in that fog… he heard Buffy was back in San Francisco… staying at her mom's house… she hadn't paged him… hadn't told him she was in town… he was furious… he went to the Tenderloin… looking for Bennies…

The dealer said… "Only got heroin."

Pat didn't flinch… "Fine. Give it to me."

He didn't remember much after that… but somewhere in the haze… something in him knew… "I'm about to die again."

Somehow… he drove to Buffy's mother's house… rang the bell… Buffy answered… her face…cold… hard… heartbreak behind the eyes…

"Pat… go away. I don't want to see you anymore."

"Buffy… please… I'm dying. I need to come in…"

"No," she said…

Anger exploded inside him… "Open the gate!" he shouted… "I'm dying!"

"No… Pat… go away…"

He screamed… cursed… "You're gonna let me die?!"

She shouted back… "No, Pat… you're the one who's going to let you die!"

The words hit him like a hammer... he collapsed... sobbing... "Please... open the door..."

She shook her head... "No. Goodbye. Forever."

She shut the door.

Pat lay there on the ground... crying... eventually... he got back in his car... remembered the heroin still in the glove box... he drove to the beach... the next thing he remembered... fire trucks... police cars... paramedics hovering...

A voice said... "Okay... he's breathing again..."

But Pat's first thought wasn't... *Thank God I'm alive.* it was... *Shit... I can't even die right.*

What now? he thought... *What the hell do I do now?* he went to his mother's house... collapsed on the couch... slept for two days straight... When he woke up... he stared at the ceiling... *Am I living in hell? I don't have a next move...* the only reason he wanted to live... was gone...

Buffy... gone...

15

The Turning Point

Pat woke up on his mother's couch… time felt like it had stopped… the house was unusually quiet… he hadn't been home in weeks… his body ached from the bender he'd been on… he looked over at the coffee table… there was a pamphlet lying there… it was from a place called Campo Della Vita… in Medjugorje, Bosnia-Herzegovina… it said something about freedom from drugs… Pat was mesmerized…

Just then… his youngest brother Stephen walked into the room… they looked at each other… no hello… just silence… Pat held up the pamphlet… "Do you know where this place is?" he asked…

"Yeah… why?" Stephen replied…

"Because I want to go," Pat said…

Stephen's face went blank with shock… "Really???"

"Yes!" Pat answered firmly…

Stephen ran out of the room… like he had just won the lottery and needed to guard the ticket… a few moments later… he came back with their mother… she was excited…

"Do you really want to go to Campo Della Vita?" she asked…

"Absolutely!" Pat replied…

He didn't fully understand what he was getting into… but he knew… God was involved… Stephen explained that he… along with Maureen… Julie… and their friends Johanna and Mike… had gone on a pilgrimage to Medjugorje… apparently… they had placed Pat's picture at the cross on Apparition Mountain… and prayed for his recovery…

They had Pat call a place in St. Augustine, Florida… it was a farm where Americans who joined the community were sent… Pat made the call… then he called Buffy… he told her he'd be leaving… possibly for a few years… he asked her if she would wait for him…

His heart shattered when she said… "No… I can't do that, Pat… I hope you get well and live a great life… but I won't wait for you."

The sadness he felt was beyond belief…

Soon after… Pat's brother John Joe, and his wife Kathleen, took him to the airport… they watched *Happy Gilmore* on the plane… it had just been released… Pat found himself identifying with Adam Sandler's character… the strange part?… He was wearing a Boston Bruins jersey… just like him… it felt like a sign… a foreshadowing…

When they arrived in Florida… what nobody knew… was that Pat still had drugs on him… Bennies hidden in his socks…

The farm leaders gave Pat nine days to decide if he wanted to stay… each day… he worked on the farm… and stayed at a hotel with his brother and Kathleen at night… at the hotel… he'd take the Bennies and stay up all night… by the eighth day… he started to lose his grip… the farm leaders noticed… They told his brother… "He's on drugs."

John Joe confronted Pat… "Are you on drugs?"

Pat denied it… John Joe was furious… and scared… everyone knew… if this didn't work… Pat was going to die… or lose his mind completely…

On the ninth day… Pat went back to the farm… planning to escape the next morning… they went into the chapel… everyone knelt down to pray… Pat sat in a chair… "My knee hurts," he lied… "I'll just sit."

In truth… he was being defiant… they began to pray… "In the name of the Father… the Son… and the Holy Spirit…"

In his heart… he whispered… *Okay, God… if you're real… and you want to save me… let me know… and I'll give you my life…* immediately… a feeling of absolute love and peace washed over him… he felt sober… free… loved… it was as if a door opened… a door he had been waiting for his entire life…

It was real… God… was real… the Holy Spirit came to him… he got on his knees… and said in his soul… *God… I give my life to you.* God received his offer… and has not let him go since… even in the darkest times… when he tried everything to throw himself out of His grace… God has never let him go... that moment... July 9, 1996... was the turning point...

The next day... July 10... the farm leaders expected Pat to tell them he was leaving... they were convinced he was still on drugs... back at the hotel that night... Pat walked into the bathroom... took the drugs out of his socks... and flushed them down the toilet...

On the 10th... they went back to the farm... it was Kathleen's birthday... they made a cake for her... no one was paying attention to Pat... they were all upset... convinced he was going to leave... they sang Happy Birthday to Kathleen... clapped... smiled... Pat stood up...

"Hey everyone... I'd like to let you all know my decision..."

They bowed their heads in sadness... they thought they knew what he was going to say...

"My decision is... I would love to stay... and be a part of this community."

Silence... complete shock...

Pat walked his brother out to his car... he said... "Hey... thank you... I believe you just saved my life." He told him... "When I see you in a few years... I'll tell you what happened... but if I tell you now... you wouldn't believe me."

John Joe hugged him... "I'm proud of you," he said...

As he turned to leave, Pat yelled... "Hey, John Joe... tell Mom and the others that I love them... and I love you too..."

John Joe waved... "Okay... bye."

Pat yelled again... "And tell Buffy... that I love her..."

John Joe shook his head... "Okay... bye, Pat."

Pat watched him drive away... dust rising from his tires... he stood there... crying... then he turned... and walked back toward his new home... the farm...

16

The Hard Road to Medjugorje

Pat woke up at 5:30 a.m… July 11, 1996…

"Svegliati, Patricio… vi fare la barba… dopo andiamo la cappella…" There was a man standing over him… barking orders in Italian… Pat blinked… still foggy from sleep…

"I have no clue what you just said…" he muttered…

A young guy named Max… who had been on the farm longer… translated…

"He told you to wake up… go shave… and we go to the chapel…"

Pat groaned… still only two days sober… the man waved his hands like a traffic cop…

"Veloce!"

"What does that mean?" Pat asked…

"He wants you to hurry up…" Max replied…

Pat muttered… "Tell him to calm down, clown. I'm going…"

Max hesitated… then nervously repeated it in Italian… "Lui dice calmati, pagliaccio…"

The man's face twisted in rage… he raised his hand with that classic Italian gesture… fingers pressed together… "Eh! Imbecilli!"

Pat smirked… "Whatever, clown…" and shuffled off…

They prayed in the chapel… that peaceful connection to God returned… later… they worked all day in the fields… at dusk, someone announced… "We're playing soccer before evening prayer!"

Everyone lined up to pick teams… the captains were Marco, the angry guy from that morning…and a young man named Carlo… Pat was picked last…

"I guess you're with me," Carlo said…

The game started… Pat scored once… then twice… then again… and again… and again… Five goals!…

Carlo stared in disbelief…

"What the heck?! You know how to play soccer?"

"Obviously…" Pat replied…

Carlo grinned… "And you're a wise guy too, I see…"

"And you speak good English…" Pat shot back…

"Yes… proper English," Carlo smiled…

They shook hands…

"I've been assigned as your guardian angel while you're here," Carlo said…

"What's that?" Pat asked…

"I'm here to help you with whatever you need…"

"Cool," Pat replied…

That evening… back in the chapel… Carlo brought Marco over…

"This is Marco," he said…

Pat muttered… "Yeah… I already dealt with this guy…"

"Marco would like to apologize… for his lack of patience and anger toward you," Carlo said… "He's working on this and would like your forgiveness…"

Pat thought… *What kind of place am I in? …I could help him with his anger by kicking his ass… that'd be quicker…* but… they were in a chapel… and Pat had just had a spiritual awakening…

He extended his hand… "It's okay… don't worry about it…"

Carlo asked… "Do you want to apologize for anything, Patricio?"

Pat paused… "Nope… nothing comes to mind…"

Max whispered… "You called him a clown…"

Pat shrugged… "Nah… you must've misunderstood… I called him homie… it's street language from SF…"

Carlo sighed… "Okay, Patricio… we'll talk more when you start growing a bit…"

Pat thought… "Growing? These fools are younger than me…"

He smiled at Marco… "It's all good, homie…"

Marco blinked… then smiled awkwardly… "Homie…"

Days passed… Pat prayed daily…

"God, I'll stay here as long as You want… but please… send Buffy… Let her show up and take me home…"

Farm life wasn't so bad… Pat loved playing soccer every day… praying three times a day… Mass brought him peace… but learning Italian was brutal… and the constant emotional sharing made him want to scream… he deflected it all with comedy… found an old Russian hat… a pair of glasses with no lenses… wore them everywhere… even during serious talks… Crotty would be in stitches… and Pat just leaned in harder… still… he kept praying…

"God… send Buffy… That will be my sign…"

Then… one day… they called him into the chapel… Gilberto… Albino – the main leader – and Carlo were waiting… "We need to talk…"

Pat braced himself…

"We want to send you to our house in Bosnia… in Medjugorje… It's a tough place," they said… "Hard work… rough conditions… We send the testa dura there… the hard heads… We believe you need to grow up… or you'll go back to the old life… Are you willing to go?"

Pat hesitated… "Can Crotty come with me?"

"No… you need to go alone…"

Pat asked for a night to think…

That night… he lay in bed… crying in the dark… *Please, Buffy… come get me… If I go to Bosnia… I might never come back… God… please… let her hear me…*

The next morning… he woke to the rooster's call… and felt a deep peace wash over him… at breakfast… he told Carlo… "I'll go…"

Carlo lit up… "You're my racehorse, man… I'm betting on you…"

"You leave tomorrow," they said…

It felt too fast… but there was no turning back…

The next day… Gilberto pulled up in a van with an American… a guy named Adam who had played professional basketball for a few years… fell into addiction after his career… but now had a few years sober…

"I'll be your new guardian angel," he told Pat…

As they were loading the van… Carlo came running out with a box… "Here… this is for you. It came from San Francisco…"

Inside were letters from Pat's family… a pair of Adidas soccer cleats… and rosary beads… there was a note… "Go win, Pat. Love, Buffy."

Pat was overwhelmed…

"Let's go," Adam said… "No time for crying…"

As they drove toward the airport… Pat stared out the window… heart breaking… he whispered… "Please, God… help me find my way…"

And the journey continued…

17

The Visit

After leaving Florida… and heading toward Medjugorje… Pat was caught between excitement and sadness… excited to see what this experience would bring… but heartbroken when he realized… he would probably never see Buffy again… He had to let go… move on… start a new life in Europe…

He arrived in Medjugorje in August 1996… the Bosnian War had ended only months before… but the scars were everywhere… soldiers from every flag patrolled the streets… tanks rolled by… helicopters thudded overhead… and orphans… so many orphans… so many people had died…

Medjugorje had become a global beacon for Catholics… ever since 1981… when a group of Croatian children claimed to see the Blessed Virgin Mary on a hillside… now… books… documentaries… pilgrimages… tens of thousands flooded this tiny town… it felt like Catholic Disneyland… but underneath the spectacle… was something real…

Pat stayed at a place called Campo Della Vita… it was run by an Italian nun named Sr. Elvira… she wasn't like any nun Pat had ever met… her eyes blazed with something otherworldly… love… mercy… she could pierce your soul with a glance… and lift it, too… She taught the boys how to live… through prayer… hard work… sacrifice… and honesty…

Each morning started at 5:30 a.m… they climbed the mountain… prayed as the sun rose over the valley… after breakfast came the chores… cooking… cleaning… dishwashing… Pat's jobs: dishes and bathrooms… which he hated… but his actual labor was in the rock pit… which he loved…

Swinging a sledgehammer… breaking stones… pushing wheelbarrows over planks… they were building things …churches, orphanages, homes… and something was being rebuilt inside Pat, too…

Evenings were for chapel and sharing… all in Italian… he had no choice but to learn…his Croatian friend, Cuke, and John Paolo helped him… by year's end… he could speak and understand pretty well…

One morning… while elbow-deep in dishwater… a woman joined him… praying the rosary while she scrubbed… Viska… one of the original visionaries… she had seen the Blessed Mother… spoken with her… and here she was… washing dishes next to Pat… he couldn't believe it… Out of thousands who came just to glimpse her… she stood by him… like it was nothing…

She looked at him… smiled softly…

"Patricio," she said, "do you know the Blessed Virgin Mary has a special love for you?… That God has called you by name?"

Pat had heard words like that before… but not like this… not with this certainty… this love… and in that moment… he believed her… Still… there were dark days…

One morning… scrubbing toilets… exhausted… sore… homesick… he wondered… *Have I made a mistake coming here?*

He missed home… his family… Buffy… what if his mother died while he was gone?… his sister Mary was running Java Beach alone… what if she needed him? He was also sad that he wouldn't be able to attend his brother Daniel and Tina's wedding…

Then it happened… a voice…inside his own head… clear… direct… not his own… "Clean the toilets, Pat."

"What?…" Again…

"Clean the toilets, Pat."

Then a third time…

"You clean the toilets… and I will take care of everything else."

Pat froze… heart pounding… this was no hallucination… he was sober now… and this… was something real…

That night… he made a little prayer box… wrote down every fear… every hope… every person he loved… slipped each folded paper inside… and made a deal with God… He would clean the toilets… break rocks… feed the animals… wash dishes… he would fast… pray… help others…

he would change... and in return... God would take care of Buffy... his family... Java Beach...

All of it...

A year later... his family visited... they told him everything was okay... even Buffy... she was finishing her last year at Smith College... no sign she wanted to see him... but she was okay... and that was enough...

Then one day... in the chapel... John Paulo approached...

"We're transferring you to a house in Italy... less physical work... more spiritual focus... Would you be willing?"

Pat asked for time...

Weeks passed...

One morning... in the Adoration chapel... Pat prayed... "God... I'll go wherever You want... Italy... Africa... Brazil... Guatemala... I'll become a Franciscan... I'll serve the poor... just tell me where to go..."

Then... he pulled out a photo of Buffy from his Bible... held it up... "But if it's Your will... I would rather marry her... live in San Francisco... raise kids... stay sober... help others..."

He set the photo down... "...but Your will be done, not mine... Fiat voluntas Tua."

The next day... he was called to the office... "You have a visitor." Pat's heart stopped... could it be his brother? a friend from San Francisco?... They led him toward the chapel... and then... he saw her... Buffy...

He ran to her... she ran to him... they embraced... so tightly... joy exploded through his chest... They sat in the dining hall... granted a private visit... Pat looked at her hands... looked into her eyes... and asked... "Will you marry me?"

Buffy smiled... tears in her eyes... and said,... "Yes."

The greatest word he had ever heard...

Pat packed his things... Buffy would meet him back in San Francisco... she flew back with her friend, Lindsay, who she traveled with... he boarded the plane... beaming... During the flight... the attendant came by... "Red or white?" she asked...

"Red," he said...

One glass... then another... then another... Maybe I can drink like a normal person now... he thought... I'm religious... I've changed... I should be okay… Just to be safe… he closed his eyes and went to sleep… the pilot's voice came over the intercom… "Welcome to San Francisco."

At the airport… Buffy was waiting… so was his family… he climbed into Buffy's car… they embraced again… grateful… overflowing… then… Buffy's face changed…

"I have really bad news," she said…

Pat tensed…

"What is it?"

"I wasn't supposed to tell you yet… but I have to…"

She hesitated… tears welled… "Mikey was supposed to pick you up today… but there was an accident at work… he's on life support…"… Her voice broke… "He's not going to make it…"

And that… was Pat's first day home.

18

Stress

One of the first things Pat did when he returned to San Francisco was go to the hospital to see Mikey… he told him he loved him… said a prayer for him… Mikey couldn't talk… he was on life support… a few hours later, Pat got the call… Mikey had passed away …

Mikey was Pat's very first friend in this world… they met in first grade at the Beach Chalet soccer fields… they had been friends ever since… his first week back from Bosnia, Pat was at Mikey's funeral… he hadn't told anyone he drank the three little bottles of wine on the plane… he figured now that he was living a religious life, he could learn to drink moderately… he was happy about that because he didn't want to go back to the spiritual group that helps people with addictions… the one Doug and Frank brought him to …

He figured he'd go to church every day and work at Java Beach… that's what he did and it seemed to work… until his first Christmas back home… He figured he could have some of his favorite Irish whiskey to celebrate … huge mistake!!!

He got very drunk and Buffy was not pleased… neither were his family and friends who believed in him and were hoping he truly changed… Pat realized at that time he may need to go back to the spiritual group… he was working about 17 hours a day so he didn't really have time… but as things seemed to coincidentally happen to him… a friend named Tim from that group would get off the N Judah at 11:00 p.m. … right when Pat was closing Java Beach …

Tim worked as a security guard downtown… he said he didn't have time for the group either, but asked if Pat would like to meet up every Saturday night at this time and have a meeting… Pat thought that was a good idea… so they'd start their meeting at midnight… they would light a candle … turn off the lights … and pray the *Prayer of St. Francis of Assisi* … then they'd talk about their lives…

Tim asked if Pat ever did the spiritual steps the group suggests… Pat said, "Kind of…"

Tim laughed and said, "I guess that's why it only kind of works for you." …

Pat laughed too and said, "Yeah, I guess."…

Tim was confident Pat had done the first three steps well enough, but thought he should start writing his story out… take some personal inventory… Pat agreed… Tim gave him some paperwork and told him to get a notebook… Pat was ready to stop drinking forever, so he figured he'd give it a try…

Buffy and Pat still planned on getting married… although she was nervous about him now… he assured her that he would change and live sober…

They set the date to get married: September 5, 1998… at St. Cecilia's Church… the reception would follow at the South End Rowing Club… her mother, Cecile, was one of the first women in that club… so it was a special place…

While they waited for that day to come… Pat had so much stress on him… he had a very difficult time living in San Francisco again… the place where he had lived such a troubled life… the other stressful thing was that Java Beach was about to lose its lease… and he didn't have enough money to purchase the building…

Mr. Lee said he would offer Pat the first opportunity, but if he couldn't pay that price, he'd need to sell to someone else… the building had become quite valuable after the success of Java Beach…

19

In God's Hands

When Pat returned from Bosnia, he realized the lease for Java Beach would soon expire… he reached out to Mr. Lee to ask if he'd consider selling him the building… Mr. Lee said, "Yes"… he was ready to move back into his newly rebuilt home, the one he lost in the 1989 Loma Prieta earthquake… he gave Pat a price…it was double the market value…but to Pat, it was worth it… because Java Beach was worth saving… it had become successful, even legendary, and all the people who once told him a coffeehouse at the beach would never survive… were now wishing they had one of their own…

Pat agreed to the price and started scrambling to figure out how to make it happen… then came the gut punch… Mr. Lee called to say someone who knew Pat was trying to buy the building had offered $100,000 more… Pat was crushed… he couldn't believe someone who knew him would do that… but he learned something that day…some people don't follow the old codes… loyalty, respect… those rules are gone for most…

Desperation started creeping in… until Maureen…his sister-in-law… his brother Thomas's wife… suggested he pray a novena to St. Joseph… she said, "You'll get your sign on the ninth day"… Pat figured, why not? What did he have to lose?

Buffy's friend Monica was living on a kibbutz in Israel… so they decided to visit… he started the novena on the plane… by the third day, he was in the Old City of Jerusalem, staying at a hostel by the Jaffa Gate…

a friend back home owned Charlie's Market... his relatives had the keys to the Holy Sepulcher... Pat found the guy's cousin, Mohammed, who told him that Christians fought so much over the keys, the Muslims now held them for safekeeping...

Pat introduced himself... told him he knew Danny from way back... Mohammed looked at him and said, "You want to come in at night, when no one's there?"

Pat said yes... that night, Pat and Buffy walked into the Holy Sepulcher alone... silence... sacred stillness... they had the whole place to themselves... it was one of the most spiritual moments of Pat's life... he decided to return every morning... before sunrise... to pray the novena... he knelt at the spot where Jesus was crucified... and begged God, "Please don't let me lose Java Beach"... day after day, same prayer...

On the eighth day, he sat on the rooftop of the hostel, sipping Turkish coffee... smoking a cigarette... listening to the Muslim prayers echo across Jerusalem...he was intrigued by the devotion and the faith of the Muslims... it hit him like lightning... *Who am I to tell God what to do?*

He thought about why he was begging instead of surrendering? He didn't need control... he needed trust...

On the ninth day, he returned to the sepulcher... dropped to his knees... and whispered: "I place myself and Java Beach in your hands."

As he walked back to the hostel, he was filled with a deep, electric peace... the kind that doesn't make sense, but is... Buffy saw it right away... "Call your mom," she said. "Tell her."

Pat went to the desk and asked to make a long-distance call to San Francisco... his mom answered... he told her he got his answer... that he had surrendered Java Beach to God... and that peace filled him like a river... she was quiet... then said, "You're not going to believe this..." He braced himself...

"Java Beach is on the front page of the *Examiner* today."

"What?? Why??" he asked.

"There's a movie being made about surfing. The actors were at Java Beach. They took a picture out front."

"Okay... and what's the name of the movie?"

"*In God's Hands*."

Pat almost dropped the phone... Just hours before, he said those exact words in a prayer in Jerusalem… and now that's the name of the movie, and Java Beach is front and center?... He was stunned… filled with wonder… floating through it all… just then, the guy at the front desk reminded him he had a tour booked… so off they went… retracing the steps of Jesus' life… one sacred place after another…

At the very end of the day, the tour guide smiled and said: "We have one last stop before heading back… the House of St. Joseph."

Pat laughed to himself… of course they do… he'd spent nine days praying to St. Joseph… and here he was… standing in the home of the very saint he'd been pleading with… What else can you do in that moment but believe?... he had no choice but to trust that this whole wild, sacred, unpredictable life… was in God's hands.

20

Belfast

One day… Pat told Buffy maybe they should go live in Europe for a while… just to get settled… to reset… they could live in Belfast… where Pat's father was from… he had plenty of relatives and friends there… it always felt like a second home…

He told her about Queen's University in South Belfast… near his uncle Eugene's house… Buffy had always wanted to get her master's degree… it seemed perfect… she smiled and said it sounded like a great idea… but… for that to happen… it would take a small miracle… especially with everything going on at Java Beach…

But then… as Pat's life tended to go… the very next morning… 9:00 a.m. Mass at Holy Name… after Mass… a man in front of him turned around… Belfast accent…

"Do you know where any coffee shops are around here?"…

For a moment… Pat thought he was on *Candid Camera*… he thought maybe the guy knew who he was… and was joking… but they didn't know each other…

"What part of Belfast are you from?" Pat asked…

"The docks," the man said… "How do you know I'm from Belfast?"…

"Because my dad's from Belfast."…

Pat told him to follow him out of church… he brought him to Java Beach… they started talking… they knew many of the same people… the man… Frankie… had even helped Pat's brother John Joe get a passport years earlier… when their grandfather passed and John Joe had to leave immediately for the funeral…

Pat told Frankie that he and his fiancée had just been talking about moving to Belfast… and then Frankie said it…

"I have a house there… on the Black Mountain… huge house… two acres… overlooks all of Belfast."…

Pat could hardly believe it… they decided to go visit Belfast …

Buffy loved the school… and the house… there was hope now… hope for a different lifestyle… surrounded by family and old friends…

Before long… Buffy was enrolled for the fall semester… they married on September 5th… it was a beautiful day… a real blessing…

After their wedding in September… Pat and Buffy left for Belfast… a beautiful home… rented to them by Frankie… Pat was determined to give Buffy the life he had promised… sober… honest… out of trouble… Buffy was deep into her Master's program… political ethnic conflict… the peace deal in Northern Ireland was unfolding all around them… it was the perfect backdrop for her studies…

Pat found some spiritual meetings in South Belfast… not far from Queen's University and his uncle's house… every day he'd meet his Aunt Mary for noon Mass… then head to the spiritual gathering… finishing each day at the chapel on Falls Road… it was the life he had tried to build since he was fifteen… now thirty… and finally living the way his father had asked him to…

He was never going to drink again… that was the promise… he went down to the Lyric Theatre one day… asked if they had any plays or film classes… they said both… next thing he knew… he was doing plays… short films… they even won best short film at the Belfast Film Festival… it felt like magic…

He played indoor soccer with Jimmy… another guy from San Francisco… Jimmy had moved to Belfast after his father passed away… solid guy… good friend… then Pat met a priest from Africa… raising money for hungry children in Malawi… Pat helped him… it felt right… everything felt right…

On weekends… Pat and Buffy would travel… Donegal was their

favorite spot… peaceful… they dreamed of buying a house there… having kids… happily ever after…

But one afternoon… at the spiritual center… Pat was talking to some guys from East Belfast… he didn't realize his Celtic jersey was showing under his hoodie… they were Rangers fans… and over there… that meant war… one of them… sober for years… usually kind… turned nasty… words were exchanged…

"Let's take this outside," Pat said…

He stepped out… they slammed the door shut behind him… locked it… peeked out the blinds as he stood alone… waiting for Buffy… no cell phones back then… he waited… and waited… alone… He took it as a sign from God… that he shouldn't return to that group…

Buffy picked him up… he told her what happened… she was nervous…

"What if these thugs come after you?" she said…

Pat reassured her… he had friends on the Falls Road… they could handle anything… but that scared her… she saw something shifting in him…

"What happened to the peace? The spiritual path?" she asked…

Pat promised to stick to church and the chapel… keep it simple… and for about a month… he did… until the day the spaghetti sauce fell out of the fridge… splattered all over his brand-new Air Jordans… he stared at the red mess… and thought… *What kind of God allows this?*

He walked to the cabinet… pulled out the vodka… and drank… then he called his friends… they went down to The Beehive… he got drunk… told them about the Rangers fans… they kept drinking… then the thought hit him… *I better get home before Buffy gets there…*

Buffy was already home… she couldn't believe it… he was drunk again… she chased his friends out of the house… slammed the bedroom door… never came out… that night… Pat slept alone… and had a dream… or more properly named a nightmare!…

He was back in San Francisco… walking through the Francis Scott Key schoolyard… shadows moving around him… dark shapes… he wanted to run… but didn't want to show fear… then something shifted… he started to fly… he didn't know he could fly… but there he was… lifting off the ground… rising straight up… then he saw it… a ten-foot beast… like a giant panther... it lunged at him... almost grabbed his feet... terrified... he flew higher... to the rooftop of the school... then woke up...

Drenched in sweat... he stumbled to the kitchen... his head pounding... his hands shaking... there was a glass of vodka on the sink... if he drank it... the hangover would go away... he lifted it to his lips... but the terror of the beast stopped him...

He threw the vodka down the drain... dropped to his knees... and prayed...

"God... please save me..."

He didn't understand the dream... but he knew it was a warning... that morning... May 7, 1999... Pat stood in the kitchen... alone...

Buffy woke up... not a word... she left for school... and Pat sat the whole day... on the Black Mountain... he knew she was going to leave him... he couldn't blame her... but he couldn't shake the dream... the beast... was it real?... was this more than just about drinking?... was something after his soul?...

Buffy still hadn't spoken to Pat that next morning, May 8th... She had school... but Pat didn't want to sit on that mountain again all day... thinking about the beast from his dream... or what he had done to the life they were building... he asked her to drop him at the city center... halfway down the hill... she finally broke the silence...

"Pat," she said, "What do you plan on doing with your life?"...

He didn't know how to answer... and he told her the truth...

"I don't know."

She said, "Can I say something to you?"

He said, "Yeah."

Then she asked, "Promise you won't get mad? Or act violent?"

"Of course," Pat said... surprised...

She took a breath and said... "I think you're a coward."

Pat laughed... actually laughed...

"I thought you were gonna say something serious," he said... "We both know I'm not a coward. You can call me a lotta things, but not that. I'm not afraid of anything...and you know that."

She nodded... "Yes, I know, Pat. You're not afraid of fighting people... even full barrooms... you're not afraid of having guns pulled on you... or overdosing... you're not afraid of dying... and that's exactly what makes you a coward."

Pat went quiet...

Buffy continued... "You're afraid of living, Pat. You're afraid of living a good and sober life. You can't even live for me... or your family... or anyone who loves you. You're on a death mission. I'd be impressed if you could live sober. That would make you brave... but this? This is cowardice... and I'm not sticking around for it."

Her words... cut deeper than anything he'd ever heard... because they were true...

Pat told her, "Take me to the meeting."

She gave him a look... "Why? So you can fight those guys again?"

"No," he said. "I want to go fight for my sobriety... for you... for my family... for me."

He went to the meeting that day... sat right next to the Rangers fans... they shook hands... Pat told them he was there to stay sober...and nobody was gonna stop him... he kept going back... every day... made some good friends from North Belfast—Irish Catholic guys who were into boxing and football... they brought him to meetings near Cave Hill... where his dad's family home was...

Pat started walking Cave Hill every day before the meetings...recalling the days of his youth... thinking about his father's tale of the banshee's cry ... trying to find the truth inside him... trying to be brave the way Buffy meant it...

One day, one of the lads asked why he could never stay sober... Pat told him he'd been trying since he was fifteen... seven rehabs... halfway houses... prayer meetings... Masses... still, he always ended up drinking... He asked if Pat had done the spiritual work...the whole thing... Pat admitted he had skipped a few things...

"Like what?" the lad asked...

"Like telling the truth about my life."

"Then go do it. All of it. There's a priest in Newcastle."

Pat didn't want to... but he was willing now... they went the next week... Pat sat with the priest... confessed everything... no holding back... even the parts that made him sick with shame... the priest listened... then said... "You need to go back to America... make peace with your past...

and when you do, you can come back to Ireland…but you can't hide here… you need to face it… that's how you'll be free…"

He sent Pat to the hill where St. Patrick used to pray… told him to give his life to God there… so he did… no matter what happened next, he was His…

Pat came home and Buffy said he looked different… brighter… like something had changed inside him… it had… he told her what the priest said… she agreed…they would go back to America after she graduated… start over… but right this time…he hasn't had a drink or drug since May 7 1999…

21

The Return to The City

When they returned to San Francisco… Pat's mom said Java Beach needed him… his sister, Mary, wanted to go back to work at UCSF…his friend, Kevin, was helping Mary landed a city job … it was time for Pat to get to work… he went straight to work…seven days a week…

He'd go to the 6:25 a.m. Mass at St. Cecilia… then work… then meetings… every single day… a year into it… he still hovered on the edge of the program… unsure if he could really stay sober for good…

That's when he met Wirt and the boys… they were serious… they lived and breathed recovery… they didn't play around… Wirt helped Pat understand the hopelessness of alcoholism… and the necessity of daily spiritual living… helping others… being of service…

Pat went all-in… led Bible studies… volunteered in jails… hospitals… rehabs…was hand picked by a meditation instructor named Micky who ran the Tigers Cave group… ran neighborhood cleanups… built parks… people started noticing… Supervisor Fiona Ma… Captain Keith Sanford…

Pat started helping with political campaigns at Java Beach… Gavin for mayor… Kamala for DA… he was finally in good standing with the world… all this time… Buffy and Pat were trying for children… nothing yet…

One day some born-again friends asked if they could pray over him… it was outside his comfort zone…but he said yes… the next week… Buffy told him she was pregnant…

Pat couldn't believe how blessed his life was… he found himself at

Catholic Charismatic prayer groups… became a born-again Catholic… he thought he understood how God worked… if he just kept praying… helping… doing the work… everything would stay good… perfect even…

22

Kevin, Our Angel

Buffy went to work as a private investigator… she was also the political editor for *The Irish Herald*… writing about the Northern Ireland peace agreement…and she started helping an overwhelmed Pat at Java Beach… they had been married for six years… but still had no children…

Then one morning… Pat woke up to Buffy shaking him… her eyes wide… her voice filled with joy…

"Pat! I'm pregnant!"…

Their first child was due on March 17…St. Patrick's Day… but something went wrong… Buffy was diagnosed with preeclampsia… the doctors said they had to induce the baby a month early… a terrifying experience… On February 14, their beautiful baby Kevin was born… Valentine's Day…

Kevin had to stay in the premature birth ward… Pat prayed day and night… please, God, let him live… he made it… eventually… they took their beloved Kevin home… lived above Java Beach… every morning, Kevin's smiling face would greet everyone who came in… he was the neighborhood baby…

He went to preschool down the block on Lawton… started playing micro soccer… Pat trained him every day… then he was offered a spot at the French American school… they accepted… before his first day… Pat told Buffy…

"Don't tell anyone I'm a soccer coach… they'll ask me to coach…"

She gave him a look… "I think you should… but okay…"

Pat just wanted to enjoy watching the games… at the school picnic… they set up small soccer goals…

"Who wants to play?" the teachers asked…

So many kids raised their hands… Pat thought to himself… I think I'll like this school… within ten minutes… Kevin had scored fifteen goals…

A French father turned and asked,… "Who is this boy's father?"

"I am, sir."

The man nodded… "Okay… you are the new coach."

Pat laughed… "How do you know I'm a soccer coach?"

The man smirked… "Any child who plays like this… was trained by one of his parents… and by the way you're dressed… it's you."

Pat looked down at his Adidas gear… his swag had given him away… and so… Kevin's passion for soccer began…

23

The Second Blessing

Pat couldn't believe how blessed his life had become… with the arrival of Kevin… watching his brilliance… his greatest dreams were coming true… then one morning… Buffy came to him with the news… she was pregnant again!!!…

Wow!… so happy… so blessed…

Conor was in no rush to meet them… he was so content inside Buffy's womb… three weeks late… finally… around Thanksgiving… it was time… they rushed to the hospital… excitement… nerves… gratitude…

In the waiting room… Pat met a gang member from the Mission district… young… tough… but something in his eyes… they started talking… Pat shared his story… told him how Jesus had transformed his life… the young man listened… then asked…

"Can you pray for me?"

Pat placed his hands on the kid's head… prayed the Jesus Miracle Prayer… right there… in the waiting room… midway through the prayer… chaos… Buffy's best friend Monica came running out…

"Pat! Get in here! The baby is coming!!!"

Pat finished the prayer… sprinted inside… just in time… moments later… Conor arrived… big beautiful eyes… staring right at Pat… as if to say… "Oh… so you're the guy I've been hearing talk this whole time…"

Shortly after… the two Kevins arrived… their little Kevin… and Buffy's dad… they had Bill's Burgers from Clement Street… poor Conor…

all he got was breast milk… funny how he still loves Bill's Burgers to this day…

Conor was just like Kevin… an incredible athlete… a wizard on the soccer field… fearless… determined… they had a video… his first micro soccer game… Children's Playground… Golden Gate Park… Conor saying Kevin told him… "Rip the hearts out of the Grizzlies by scoring tons of goals… Kill them… (but not really kill them)… Score in the last seconds… that's how you rip their hearts out…"

Pure competitor… just like his brother… what a journey it had been…

24

The Cycle of Life

After being blessed with Kevin and Conor, Pat couldn't imagine how life could get any better… until one day… Buffy announced the greatest news… she was pregnant again… the baby was due in September…

Kevin was six… Conor was three… both were ecstatic…

They had just moved down the block… to a house that straddled two streets… the Great Highway… or La Playa… depending on which side of the house you stood on… a strange setup… but it was home…

September came… and just like Conor… this baby was in no rush to arrive… one afternoon… as Pat sat in the living room… he heard a bell from a fire truck… he looked out the window… it was Engine 23… his brother John Joe was on the rig with his crew…

"Hey! Did you guys have the baby yet?" John Joe called out…

Pat shook his head… "No… he's too comfortable in there… taking his time…"

John Joe laughed… "Well… we just had training on how to deliver a baby… so if you need us… just holler!"

They both laughed…

Kevin and Conor were thrilled to see their uncle on the fire engine… the crew blasted the horn for them… and drove off…

A week later… Buffy went to the hospital for a check-up… the doctor said there were still no signs of labor… so she went home… she figured… why not take the boys to their favorite soccer shop in the Mission?… they needed new cleats…

Meanwhile… Pat was in the backyard when his phone rang… it was his sister, Christianne… Her voice was heavy… "Hey, Pat… I have really sad news…"

His stomach dropped…

"Aunt Kathy is at UCSF… she doesn't have much time left… if you want to say goodbye… you should come now…"

Aunt Kathy… she wasn't just an aunt… she had practically raised him…his cousin, McKenzie, was his same age… because of her… he got to experience things his siblings never did… Hawaii… Disneyland… Pebble Beach… fancy restaurants… her home in St. Francis Woods had been his escape… from the chaos of the Lower Sunset District…

Aunt Kathy was special… Pat called Buffy… "I need to go to the hospital," he told her…

"Okay…" she said… "I'll see you at home soon…"

"How are you feeling?" he asked…

"Not great… but I'll be okay…"

Pat drove to UCSF… when he walked into the hospital room… his cousin Christy was there… she looked up… her eyes full of grief… "Go ahead, Pat… say goodbye to Mom…"

He stepped forward… took Aunt Kathy's hand… "Aunt Kathy… I just want to thank you… for everything… I love you… I will miss you…"

Christy asked… "Did your baby come yet?"

"No… not yet… but Buffy just told me she's not feeling well… she's heading home…"

Christy turned to her mother… "Hey Mom… Pat needs to go… Buffy needs him… they're having a baby soon…" Aunt Kathy turned her eyes toward him… she couldn't speak… but he could feel what she was saying…

I love you, Pat… go home to Buffy…

He leaned down… kissed her forehead… "Oh… one more thing, Aunt Kathy…" he whispered… "I'm sorry… for all the trouble I caused you…"

Her eyes twinkled… *Oh boy… you were a problem, Pat…* but beneath it… he felt her saying… *You know I forgive you…* Christy squeezed his arm…

"Pat… get out of here… go have that baby…" He hugged her… and left…

As soon as he got in the car... he called Buffy... "How are you feeling?" he asked...

"Okay... can you grab some drinks at Judahlicious for me and the boys?"

Pat cried the whole way down Judah Street... he pulled up... grabbed the drinks... and drove home... when he arrived... Kevin and Conor were outside... jumping up and down with excitement...

"The baby is coming, Daddy!" they shouted...

Pat smiled... "Yes... very soon, he will be here..."

"No, Daddy! He's coming now! Mommy is on the floor—she needs you!"

Pat ran upstairs... Buffy was on the floor... in pain...

"Get me to the hospital, Pat," she groaned...

"Okay... let's go," he said, moving to help her... she cried out... dropped to the floor again... she couldn't move...

"I need to call 911," he said...

"You better not!" she warned... "I'll be so mad... just get me to the hospital!" Pat immediately called her best friend, Monica... she was hosting a Rosh Hashanah dinner...

"Monica... I need you here...now."...

She must've had a teleportation machine... because she arrived immediately... she knelt beside Buffy... "How do you want us to get you to the hospital?"

Buffy screamed in pain... Monica reached down... her face changed...

"Oh my God... I can feel the baby's head! He's coming now! CALL 911!"

Pat grabbed his phone... moments later... Engine 23 was at the door... he knew every firefighter by name... but John Joe wasn't there... they rushed inside... Buffy was on the floor...

Pat pleaded... "Please... let's get her to the hospital!" the lead paramedic shook his head... "We're having the baby right here. He's coming out."

Pat felt like fainting... one firefighter held his hand... another held Buffy's... somehow... in between Buffy's screams... and Pat's whispered Hail Marys... one of them started making small talk...

"You ever had a Java Beach sandwich? They're amazing..." The lead paramedic's voice cut through the noise...

"We have a blue baby…"

…Silence…

"Give me the scissors…" he commanded… "The cord is around his neck…"

Pat's heart stopped… he snipped the cord… "Buffy… push!"… with a guttural scream… she gave one final push… and at 8:23 PM… September 18, 2009… their beautiful baby boy Dylan was born…

They placed him on Buffy's chest… he was perfect… everyone celebrated… hugging… crying… downstairs… a crowd had gathered… people taking pictures… cheering… Buffy's father had appeared out of nowhere…

At the hospital… as they stepped into the elevator… Pat noticed someone beside him… Gavin Newsom… mayor of San Francisco…

"Gavin?"

"Pat?"

They laughed… "What are you doing here?" Pat asked…

"My wife just had a baby," Gavin said…

Pat grinned… "So did we."

Gavin glanced at the swarm of emergency workers outside the room… "I thought I had security… what's going on here?"… Pat chuckled… "That's my family."

Later that night… as Pat sat beside Buffy… watching her cradle their newborn son… his phone rang… it was John Joe… "I heard Engine 23 delivered Dylan," he said…

"Yeah… can you believe it?"

"I wasn't there because…" he paused… "I was at UCSF… holding Aunt Kathy's hand."

Pat closed his eyes…

"She passed," John Joe said softly… "Right after I told her Dylan was born."

That night… Pat witnessed the cycle of life… birth and death… love and grief… family and faith… and he wondered… *Was this the face of God?*

With gratitude and wonder… he pondered these things in his heart…

25

I Know Why the Banshee Cried

In May of 1996… Pat sat across from Buffy in the café at Graceland… he was 28…hopeful…sober for the first time in years … he had a vision of what life could be… a normal, quiet life… a good life… married to Buffy… raising children… coaching … watching games… telling bedtime stories…

He wanted to be the kind of father he had loved… the kind that made life feel safe… he dreamed of a home by the ocean… and a life built around love, service… and story… that dream… eventually came true…

They were living on the Great Highway… the wind shook the windows… the sea mist painted the glass… they had three sons now… Kevin, Conor, and Dylan… and Pat was coaching soccer and basketball… just like he always wanted…

Being a father made Pat's life feel complete… every night before bed, he told the boys stories… just like his father once told him… tales of Ireland… of the Maguire kingdom in Enniskillen… of Seamus the leprechaun… and of the crying banshee… the banshee scared the boys sometimes… but Pat assured them… "She's good… she cries because she loves us… "she watches over noble families," he'd say… "and leaves silver combs behind so you know she was there…"

"But why does she cry?" Kevin once asked…

Pat didn't know… his father had never told him the answer… in the summer of 2011… Buffy had an idea…

"Let's take the boys to Ireland…"

The dream came alive again… the boys were buzzing…

"Are we going to take our castle back from the guys who stole it?" Kevin asked…

Pat smiled… "Yes… we're going to restore the kingdom…"

They landed in Belfast… stayed with Frankie up on Black Mountain… his back garden looked out over the city… but Frankie also had a place in Cushendall… a quiet spot near the sea… from there, the journey began…

They drove north through Ballymoney… under the dark hedges… those haunting, twisting trees… to the ruins of Dunluce Castle, hanging over the sea… to the Giant's Causeway, where the stones seemed to hum with myth…

They visited Pat's cousins, the Kerrs, in Ballycastle… and finally… made their way to Enniskillen… to the Maguire Castle…

Kevin insisted on wearing his full Celtic soccer kit… it was pouring rain… but Kevin didn't care…

"I have to play in front of the castle," he said… so they did…

When they arrived, they found the castle had been turned into a museum… Pat looked around… marched up to the security guard…

"You're doing a great job watching over the castle," he said… "We'll be back in a bit to take it back… keep it clean and tidy…"

The guard blinked… unsure if Pat was joking, serious, or touched by something otherworldly… Buffy rolled her eyes… the boys were grinning… completely convinced they were reclaiming their ancestral kingdom…

Buffy, Conor, and Dylan headed back to the car to warm up… Pat and Kevin stayed… they passed the ball in the rain… just the two of them… until two young men stepped out from the hedges… Rangers fans… about twenty years old… they looked at Kevin's Celtic gear… tension hung for a beat… but then they heard Pat's voice…

"You're Americans?" one of them said…

"We are."… The mood shifted… they smiled… started chatting… then kicking the ball to Kevin… Kevin stunned them with a bicycle kick goal… they stared…

"How old is he?"

"Seven," Pat replied…

"Magic!"

They played together for nearly an hour... no politics... no rivalry... just football in the rain... when it was time to leave... the Rangers fans walked them to the car...

"He's going to be a pro someday," one said...

Pat nodded... "I agree."

That night, they returned to Cushendall... and ducked into a little pub called Johnny Joe's... inside... glowing fire... pints on the table... pipe smoke in the air... and near the hearth... an old seanchai... a storyteller... Padraig Óg O'Neil... from Tyrone... paddy cap... long-stem pipe... eyes that flickered with something ancient... he began to speak...

He told the story of the banshee... but not just any story... it was the exact tale Pat's father once told him... every word... every twist... Buffy leaned over...

"The boys are getting scared... I'm going to take them home..."

Pat stayed... he had to know... he needed to understand... Padraig Óg looked into the fire... then into Pat's eyes...

"The banshee connects this world to the other world... she protects noble families... watches the line... she cries when death draws near... but her cry is not just grief... it's love... it's remembrance... her song is made of sorrow... and joy... because she knows what most have forgotten... that this world is under a spell... the true kingdom lies beyond the veil... this is the land of trial... shadow... forgetting... but the other world... is light... memory... truth... the banshee cries when a soul returns home... her cry opens the path... she weeps for us here... who still remain under the spell..."

Pat didn't speak... he felt it... deep in his blood... deeper than memory...

"The High King is coming," Padraig Óg whispered... "He will rescue the nine hostages... he will restore the true kingdom... but only when the seven laws are remembered..."

Pat didn't ask what they were... not yet... he just closed his eyes... and listened to the story ... the cry that echoed from Graceland to Cushendall... from a boy's dream to a father's truth... it was a cry of homecoming... and of promise... a sacred sound that said... the kingdom is real... and it will return...

When they were going to sleep that night in Cushendal… the wind was howling and rain was lashing… the wind coming through the windows made a high pitched noise… it sounded like a whistle… the boys huddled up in bed asked … "Daddy is that the banshee crying? "

Pat said, "I'm not sure…it could be."… The boys went off to sleep after their long day… Pat knew that none of his tales were true…just good Irish fun… but what was true is that Kevin made friends with Rangers fans while wearing his Celtic gear… all in front of the castle…as they say in Belfast "Pure magic!"…

It was a trip to remember…

26

The Window

When they returned to San Francisco... they had just moved from their apartment above Java Beach... to a spot down the block... at Kirkham and La Playa... more room for the babies... more room for breath...

One night... the doorbell rang around 12:15 a.m.... it was one of the guys from the spiritual group that Pat let gather at Java Beach late on weekends... what started as two friends meeting after the streetcar... had grown into something more communal...

That night... the guy said... "Are you the owner of Java Beach?"

Pat said, "Yes."... The guy continued...

"You better get down there... someone just threw a rock through the window..."

Pat felt fire in his chest... he was furious... he turned to Buffy... "I'm gonna go down there and beat the hell outta the guy..."

Buffy begged him not to... but Pat couldn't hear her... he was halfway out the door... halfway down the block... when he caught himself... stopped... and prayed...

"God... please forgive me for my anger... Java Beach is in your hands... I'm just the caretaker..."

Instant peace... the same peace he had felt once before... in Jerusalem... by the time Pat arrived... the police had the guy in custody...

An officer looked at him and said... "You're awfully calm..."

She had no idea...

People were already sweeping up the broken glass... the kindness of strangers… it humbles you… Pat figured he'd be there all night… a huge window… totally shattered… but he called Ted… his handyman… just to see if he might be awake…

Ted answered… said he was at 7-Eleven on 46th and Judah… just a few blocks away… he told Pat he had a piece of plywood in his truck… "about the size of your window…"

It was exactly the size… no cutting needed… four 2x4s… also the exact length needed…

By 1:00 a.m.… the window was boarded… and Pat was walking back home… feeling calm… covered… and protected…

The next morning… they walked the beach… Buffy… the boys… their chocolate cocker spaniels… Elvis and Bobo…

A hot… sunny Sunday… Pat told her the whole story… she listened in amazement… then said… "Shouldn't we try to get the window fixed today? It'll look terrible all boarded up on a day like this…"

Pat said, "Too expensive… it's Sunday… they'll charge double…"

Buffy said, "What about Window Man Tom? Maybe he knows someone…"

Pat thought… *no way… he's union… works downtown on high-rises…* but Pat had learned not to argue with Buffy… so he called Java Beach from his little flip phone… a staff member answered…

Pat asked, "Is Tom around?"…

She said, "He's next in line…"

Pat nearly dropped the phone… Tom got on the line… Pat told him what happened…

Tom said, "I saw it…"

Pat asked if he knew anyone who could fix it on a Sunday…

Tom said, "No… but I happen to have a window in the back of my truck… it might be the right size…"

It was… exactly…

Pat told Buffy… She was stunned… but then her smile faded…

"It needs to be double-paned tempered glass" she said…

Pat's heart sank… he asked Tom… "Is it double-paned tempered glass?"

Tom said, "It is."… and just like that… of course it was… Tom installed it immediately…

By the time they got home from their walk… Java Beach had a brand new window… Pat asked how much he owed him… Tom said… "Nothing… it's on me…"

Because when something is placed in God's hands… miracles follow… and when blessings like this arrive… what could ever go wrong?...

Hmm…

27

The Fire

May 12, 2012... it was an exceptionally beautiful spring day... the kind that made people stop and breathe it all in... the kind that made a soul believe in miracles...

Pat had just celebrated his sobriety birthday on May 7... thirteen years without alcohol or narcotics... He was living the dream... three beautiful, athletic boys... Kevin... 8... Conor... 5... Dylan... 2... a marriage to the woman he loved... three prosperous businesses... the perfect house on the Great Highway... just a block from the original Java Beach...

That morning... the sun was out... butterflies danced in the air... the scent of star jasmine carried on the breeze... Kevin had scored six goals in his soccer game the night before... and today... today was special... it was the championship match in Palo Alto... but first... a birthday party...

As Pat stood there... watching his boys... watching his life... he thought... *How did I become so blessed?...*

For years... he had given back... volunteering at San Bruno jail once a week... running two book studies for recovering addicts... leading the prayer group and Bible study at church... president of the Christian Businessmen's Fellowship of Daly City... coaching six soccer teams... three basketball teams ... all champions... building the most competitive soccer club in San Francisco...

He was living by spiritual principles...was a member of The Tigers Cave meditation group ... helping others... when someone would ask how he was doing… his answer was always the same… "I'm abundantly blessed."…

They were driving down Sunset Boulevard… heading for Highway 280… the perfect family on the perfect day… then Kevin spoke up from the back seat… "I don't feel well…"

Pat turned to look at him… maybe nerves… unusual for Kevin… but it was the championship…

Buffy was driving… Pat told her to pull over at Vicente and Sunset… Kevin stepped out… took three steps… and collapsed… Pat ran to him… scooped him up… his eyes rolled back in his head…

"Buffy… let's go… hospital… now…"

He held Kevin in his arms as they sped through traffic… the sun still shined… the jasmine still bloomed… but the world had changed…

They made it to California Pacific… Kevin was losing consciousness… Pat ran into the ER with his son in his arms… the medical staff grabbed Kevin… put him on a gurney… cut off his soccer jersey… oxygen mask on… rushed him inside…

Pat stayed with Conor and Dylan… trying to be strong… they were terrified… and so was Pat… he prayed… *God… I know you will watch over Kevin… I trust you… I trust you…*

Buffy came out… "They have him breathing… but there's a mass on his brain…"

The world tilted…

No… no…

They needed to go to Stanford Children's Hospital immediately… emergency brain surgery… Buffy went in the ambulance… Pat drove the boys… kept talking… kept praying… *Everything will be okay… everything will be okay…*

The surgery… the waiting… the terror…

The doctor came out… "We got most of it… but not all"… then came the oncology team…

"Stage 4 medulloblastoma… rare brain cancer in children…"

Pat walked into Kevin's room… held his hand… "Kevin… we're gonna have to walk through some fire… but when we come out… we'll shine like gold… God will heal you… and He will be glorified through us… All will see that we have a mighty God…"

Kevin... the boy with the big... bright smile... his face twisted with pain... he looked at his father and said... "Okay, Daddy... but when can I play soccer again?"

Pat swallowed the lump in his throat...

"Soon, I hope..."

Kevin fought... he fought with everything he had... more surgery... extreme chemotherapy... they even went to Israel for cutting-edge treatment... but on August 4, 2013... as Kevin lay in Buffy's arms in their bed at home... his breath grew shallow... his oxygen levels dropped...

Pat turned to God...

"I can't watch him suffer anymore... please take him from this pain God..."

He called Conor and Dylan... "Come kiss Kevin goodbye... he's going to heaven now... but we'll see him there..."

They kissed their brother... whispered their goodbyes... Pat leaned in... "Kevin... if you can hear or see God... go to Him now... when my time comes... I'll find you there... I promise... I'll take care of your brothers... I'll take care of Momma..."

Kevin turned his head toward his father... took three breaths... and was gone...

Buffy held him in her arms... a mother cradling her lifeless son... like the Pieta... Mary holding Jesus... they wept beyond belief...

Buffy asked for time alone with Kevin... she combed his hair... dressed him in his soccer uniform... then the van came... to take his little body to the morgue...

Buffy asked to be alone... Pat took Conor and Dylan to the park... they shot baskets... the sun still shined... the jasmine still bloomed... and he realized... he had asked his 9-year-old son to walk through fire... but it was Pat... it was Pat who had to keep walking... because the gates of hell opened on May 12, 2012... and the fire never stopped...

28

Let It Be

In the first year after Kevin passed away... Pat went into a state of ontological shock... nothing made sense anymore... questions he had never asked before came flooding in...

Who am I?... Where did I come from?... What am I doing?... Where am I going?... What is life?... What is the purpose?... Is God real?... If so... is God good?...

Does prayer even matter?... Does anything even matter?... Have I imagined this strange life I've lived?... Was any of it even real?...

One morning... after Buffy and the boys left for school... Pat broke down... he cried out to God... and then he stopped... because maybe God couldn't even hear him... he thought about Medjugorje... Bosnia and Herzegovina... he remembered when Viska... one of the visionaries... told him the Virgin Mary had a special love for him... that God had called him by name... that He had a plan for his life...

Pat had never doubted it... until now...

He began to cry... a guttural... aching cry...

Mary... are you real?... Do you really have a special love for me?... Did God really call me by name?...

He begged her...

I need you to come to me and tell me... because I'm losing my faith... I don't even believe my own story anymore... maybe my imagination was too big... maybe it was all wishful thinking... Could my whole life have been a farce?... If there is a God... does He hate me?... Am I being punished?... Have I been cursed?...

He thought about his near-death experience in 1993...

Did I never really come back?... Was I actually living in hell?...

He cried louder...

Please Mary... come to me... I need you to stand right in front of me and tell me you and Jesus are real... Does God love me?... Does He have a plan for my life?... I need you now... If you don't come... I'll take it as my answer... that my life is just a lie... nothing... Are you coming?... Can you hear me?"...

Nothing... really... nothing... Just like when he prayed for Kevin to be healed... and he had believed... believed that God would heal him... believed that faith could move mountains... believed that whoever asks shall receive... he believed...

Was he wrong?... Was it all fake?... Were the atheists right?... Had he been a fool?... He sat there... waiting... Nothing...

So that's it, huh... *How am I supposed to live... not believing in God?... my whole sobriety was built on belief in God... Would I have to lie to people now?... pretend God hasn't abandoned me... when, clearly, he has?... why would I defend such a God?... If God really wanted me to follow Him... why let me go through this?... Was God even a He?...*

So many questions... Pat was completely... lost...

The next day was strange... he had never lived a single day without believing in God... How was he supposed to now?... His thoughts became bizarre... even blasphemous... but how could there be blasphemy if there was no God?...

He started to wonder... about everything... all the different religions... the wars... the hatred... the scandals... *Why are some of the nicest people from other religions?... Why do Christians of different denominations read the same bible, but come to different conclusions?... What about the Gnostics?... Was the Old Testament God evil?... He seemed like a different guy from the New Testament...*

What about aliens?... the orbs I saw in Israel... after going into the pyramids in Egypt?... Were they real?... Which ones were good?... Were any good?... Pleiadians... Arcturians... Sirians... Greys... Was the world run by evil reptilian aliens?... Was the world even round?... It looked flat... Are we trapped in a dome?... Is everything... a lie?...

Maybe…

He thought about all the lies he had believed … even in his spiritual life… imagining speaking in tongues… falling out in the spirit… imagining God was speaking to him…

Are these just my own insane thoughts?…Was I was helping God?… or was I just filled with pride… and wickedness?… Maybe that's why God hates me…

He thought about all the phonies he'd seen at healing services… the same guy got out of a wheelchair three nights in a row… pretending Jesus healed him… Was everyone like that guy?…

Why would God heal someone's back pain… but let a child die of cancer?… Why heal some… but not others?… Did they tithe more money?… Did they have more faith?… If faith was all it took… why don't the people with faith go to children's hospitals… and heal the kids there?…

The questions came like hailstones… day and night…

What did I do to deserve this?… He could think of some things… but he knew people way worse than him… who never suffered like this…

He couldn't sleep… *Am I going crazy?… Maybe I've always been crazy… but doesn't God save crazy people… especially when they ask?…*

Three days of this… three days of ontological madness…

He felt so alone… no one to talk to… but still… he had to take his dogs…Elvis and Bobo…out for a walk…

On the third day… walking down San Benito Way… he saw a tiny piece of paper blowing up the street… something about it seemed… magical… it felt like it was calling him… so he chased it… a crazy man chasing a piece of paper in the wind… but he had to catch it…

He pulled the dogs along as he ran… and finally he caught it…by stepping on it… his hands shook as he picked it up… he turned it over… and read… three words… "LET IT BE"

Whoa… *Let it be…* he repeated it over and over… staring at those words… he thought about the Beatles song… *Let It Be…* he had never really listened to the Beatles… he liked country music… he thought the Beatles were some kind of hippie band… but he Googled the lyrics… and he was shocked…

Mother Mary comes to me… standing right in front of me… speaking words of wisdom… let it be…

Three days earlier… he had begged Mary to stand in front of him and tell him she was real... now here were the words... *Mother Mary comes to me... standing right in front of me...*

He sat there... stunned... an old church hymn came to mind... only God can be three days late... and still right on time...

He took the little piece of paper home... taped it to Kevin's picture... and he knew... he would have a thousand more questions... in his grief... in his loss... on this journey... but he didn't need all the answers... he only needed one thing... God is real... and He gave Pat a message through the Virgin Mary...

Let it be...

To this day... when his thoughts spiral into questions too big to answer... he remembers... and he lets it be...

29

Compassionate Friends

After the ontological shock came the ontological awakening... after the *Let it be* sign... after the realization that Pat hadn't just lost Kevin... he had lost everything he believed in... not by choice... not in rebellion... but in fire and ashes... his entire paradigm burned to the ground... leaving him standing in the wreckage... wondering what was real... and what had ever been real to begin with...

He didn't know what to think about anything anymore... but he couldn't deny that something miraculous was happening...

He had spent years in his recovery group hearing that he could have his own understanding of a Higher Power... as long as he believed in something... that had never sat well with him as a Catholic... he wrestled with it... tucked it away... told himself maybe he was there to help others find his understanding of God... maybe that was his purpose... but now... now he wasn't sure if he understood anything at all...

The first Monday after they buried Kevin... his sister Mary called and asked him to go to yoga with her... Mary understood grief in a way most people didn't... she had lost her son, Sean, at just three days old... she had carried that loss every day for years... just as she had carried Pat through so many of his own struggles... running Java Beach while he was in Europe... helping him get his footing in recovery...

Pat didn't want to go to yoga... he wanted to die... he wanted to find Kevin... but he had made a deathbed promise to his son... *I will take care of your brothers and your mother… and when my life is finished… I will find you again…*

So… reluctantly… he went…

One day turned into a week… a week turned into a month… a month into a year… every morning… he showed up… because if he could get through the morning… maybe he could get through the day… he would lay on the ground and cry… hoping no one would notice… and then… little by little… he started having conversations… deep… emotional… open conversations… and it felt safe…

It felt strange too… because before the shock… Pat would have judged these people… dismissed them… but now… now they were saving him… they were teaching him how to breathe again… literally…

He got so deep into it that he moved to the Daly City Bikram studio… where the classes were longer… where he could disappear into the heat and the silence for 90 full minutes… and he found people there too… people who knew about grief… about suffering… about finding peace in the wreckage…

And yet… his recovery group…the place that had once been his home… became harder and harder to go to… he had been someone others looked up to… and now… now he was the biggest mess in the room…

One night… a guy outright said it… "This group isn't for your kind of issues"… as if grief had an expiration date… as if Pat should have been over it… as if a father's heartbreak was something to just move on from…

His first instinct… teach him a lesson the old way… but he knew better now… he was better now… and in that moment… he realized something… the guy was right… it was time to move on…

That's when Pat found Compassionate Friends… a group for parents who had lost children… a house of sorrow… but a house where he belonged…

One Monday in Burlingame… they said they had a special guest… someone with a unique story of tragedy… loss… grief… and healing… that's when he met Tom… there was something about the man the moment Pat saw him… something in his presence… his glow… his shine… his smile… it wasn't pity in his eyes… it was understanding… it was love…

Then Tom told his story… his daughter had died at 15 months old in her crib… years later… on the tenth anniversary of her passing… his wife told him her heart was hurting... he drove her to the hospital... a few hours later... she was gone...

Then... on his middle child's 13th birthday... he heard a thud from upstairs... ran up... his son was on the floor... he got him to the hospital... and just like Kevin... they were told it was a brain tumor...

Friends and family told Tom... God wouldn't let this happen again... but 14 months later... just like Kevin... his son was gone...

Pat sat there in shock... in disbelief... this man had lived the worst nightmare three times over... and yet... somehow... he shined...

Pat came to three conclusions that night... one... this man had found a spirituality that he needed to find, or... two... the man had been driven completely mad by grief... or three... either way... Pat needed whatever he had...

After the meeting... Tom gave him a copy of his book... they talked... they became friends... Tom eventually had to move away... but they kept in touch... and there was something Tom said to him that night... something that froze him in wonder...

He said he knew two things for sure... one... that Kevin... and his wife... and his two children... had completed their mission on this earth... and ours was not complete yet... and two... that they were with us... always... closer than the people standing next to us...

Tom said... "They go everywhere with me"...

Pat didn't know what to think of that... but he knew one thing... this man had something he needed... and he was willing to go absolutely crazy to find it...

30

The Visitation

After meeting Tom... Pat knew it was time to face his spiritual life... to admit that he had been experiencing something beyond the ordinary all his life... through dreams... synchronicities... signs... and countless moments no one else could explain...

Teachers had labeled him a daydreamer... said it was a problem... but Pat's mind slipped away so far sometimes, he couldn't hear the teacher calling his name... couldn't hear classmates laughing... his grades had dropped... but now... he knew it wasn't a flaw... it was a gift.

His brainwaves often slipped into theta... that space between sleep and waking... where dreams and reality blend... where memories come alive... where the veil feels thin...

One morning... walking Elvis and Bobo... Pat drifted there again... standing on a corner when suddenly... Kevin came to him... it felt like a dream...

Kevin's voice so clear... the way he always spoke...

"Hey, Daddy!"

"Kevin!"

"It's me... do you remember these times?"

In his mind's eye... three moments appeared... Kevin at Terra Linda pool... eating watermelon... sunlight sparkling on his wet hair... Kevin on a beach in the south of France... brown Hawaiian shirt... toes buried in sand... and Kevin at halftime of a summer soccer game in the Mission

District… with Pat pouring water over his head at Garfield Park… Kevin's laughter echoing.

The memories weren't distant… they felt real… like Pat was there… transported… crystal clear… almost touchable…

"Yes, Kevin… I remember… they were beautiful moments…"

But then… sadness swept over Pat… the ache of knowing they were gone… that Kevin was gone… Kevin's smile faded… concern in his eyes…

"What's wrong, Daddy?"

"Those memories… they make me sad now…"

Kevin's tenderness was pure… "Don't be sad, Daddy… that's where I live."

Pat paused… "What do you mean?"

"I live in those moments."

"I don't understand…"

"I live in a thousand sunrises and a thousand sunsets… I say that number so you'll understand… I live in all things beautiful… all at once… If you want to find me… look at all things beautiful… that's where I am."

Tears filled Pat's eyes…

"If that's true, Kevin… I'm okay… I'll look for you in all things beautiful…"

Kevin began to float away… Pat panicked…

"Kevin, please don't go! Stay!"

He drifted further… voice echoing… "Look for me in all things beautiful, Daddy!"

And then…Pat was back… standing on the corner with his dogs… just like old days… but this time… no teacher yelling… no laughter mocking… just Pat… on Santa Ana Avenue…

The day was beautiful… a hummingbird hovered… butterflies flitted past… the scent of spring flowers filled the air…

Pat whispered… "All things beautiful… I will find you there, Kevin…"

He walked home in euphoric disbelief… knowing Kevin was with him… in every sunrise… every sunset… every beautiful moment this world still offered…

31

Goodbye, Billy

It was the first St. Patrick's Day after Kevin died... Pat went to his grave... he brought shamrocks with him and placed them gently on the stone... he stood there quietly... at first... but something inside him broke loose... the pain came up like a tidal wave... he cried... a deep... guttural cry... the kind of grief that rips through your entire body... he didn't try to stop it... he just let it out...

At some point... he must have collapsed onto Kevin's grave... because the next thing he knew... he woke up three hours later... the sun was setting... and he was disoriented... he sat up slowly... wiping his eyes...

Pat needed to clear his mind... so he drove to Lake Merced and started walking the path around it... by the time he reached the other side... it was dark... shadows stretched across the trail... he heard rustling from the bushes ahead... and then... a man stepped out... it was Billy...

Billy... his old friend from Serenity House... from years ago... who used to teach him Kung Fu... but now... he was barely recognizable... his eyes were wild... and his face was sunken... Pat could tell immediately that he was in psychosis...

Billy stared at him... his body tense... Pat said... "Hello... Billy."... but Billy didn't respond the way Pat expected... his delusions had him convinced Pat was his enemy... he started rambling... accusing him of things that made no sense...

Pat sighed... "Billy... I don't have time for this nonsense," he said... "I just came from Kevin's grave."

The moment he said Kevin's name… something shifted in Billy… his wild expression softened… he blinked… then asked… "Kevin… died?"…

He had no idea… and hearing it struck him into a rare moment of clarity… Billy told Pat he'd been homeless for three years… his family hadn't spoken to him in over fifteen… he was alone… lost in his mind… then he asked… "Can I walk the lake with you?"…

At first… Pat hesitated… part of him wanted to say no… but something in Billy's eyes made him say yes…

"Okay… but don't make me regret it," he told him…

They walked in silence for a while… then Billy finally said… "When I'm with you… I feel sane… I think it's Kevin's spirit… he's with you… isn't he?"…

Those words stayed with Pat…

The next day… he called Billy's daughter Sophia… he wanted to see if she would meet with her father… she refused… but she did tell him something… "Tell my father he's a grandfather now… I had a little girl… her name is Stella."…

Pat passed the message on to Billy… he broke down in tears… hope flickered in him for the first time in years…

Pat worked to get him off the streets and into a home… Billy started holding on to the hope that his family might forgive him someday…

They walked the lake every day after that…

A few months later… Pat had to leave for England… he was attending a soccer coaching program at West Ham United… before he left… he promised Billy he'd be back soon…

"Just a few weeks," he said…

But while he was there… he got a call from Billy's social worker…

"Pat… Billy was found unconscious on the floor of his home… he's not drunk… he has full-body cancer… we rushed him to the hospital."…

Pat immediately called Sophia… she was in Los Angeles… he told her what was happening… and she made it to her father's bedside… Sophia didn't come alone… she brought her mother… Billy's ex-wife… and little Stella… they stood around him… together… as a family…

There… at his deathbed… they found peace… forgiveness…

A few days later… Sophia called Pat… "My dad… he's holding on for some reason… I don't understand why…"

"Sophia… tell him this… if he can see a light… tell him to go to it… call out to Jesus… when my day comes… I'll do the same… and I'll find him there."

Moments later… Sophia called back… her voice stunned… "Pat… how did you know?"

"How did I know what?" Pat asked…

"He went… right after I told him… I thought about pop's last words to you before you left… 'Kevin is an angel… and he saved my soul.'"…

Tears welled in Pat's eyes… he knew… deep down… that Kevin's spirit had been with him all along… Billy had felt it too… and in his final moments… Pat wondered if Kevin had guided him home with Jesus…

Sometimes… life gives you moments you can't explain… you can only feel them… you can only see the beauty hidden in the pain…

32

Felix

Life had certainly changed after Kevin died… everything felt strange… surreal… as though Pat were walking through a dream… he was in a state of ontological shock… questioning the very fabric of reality…

During that time… a name began appearing over and over again… in conversations… in texts… on flyers… almost like it was following him… Felix Lee Lerma… a psychic medium…

At first, Pat ignored it… but the name wouldn't go away… it showed up again… and again… and again… eventually… curiosity got the better of him… he made an appointment… secretly… he kept it a secret for one simple reason… Pat is Catholic… and the voices of many devout Catholics he respected echoed in his head…

"Don't go to a medium… it's wrong… dangerous… forbidden…"

But something deeper stirred in him… a sense that maybe… just maybe… this Felix was placed on his path for a reason…

On the day of the appointment… Pat drove in silence to Baker Street in San Francisco… Felix's office was quiet… unassuming… he sat in the car for a few minutes… nervous… then he spoke aloud… to no one… and to everyone…

"Mom… Dad… Kevin… Mikey… Billy… if you guys can hear me… please come through today… Otherwise… I won't believe."

Billy was the test… Pat figured anyone could Google his story… find out about his mom… his dad… even Kevin… maybe even Mikey, his best friend who died in '97… but Billy?… no one would know about Billy…

He walked inside…

Felix greeted him with warmth… sincerity… no flash… no drama… just kindness…

"Let's begin," Felix said.

They sat… and without any prompting… Felix started…

"There's a lady here… older… holding rosary beads… Is your mother in spirit?"

Pat swallowed hard… "Yes… she is."

"Does the rosary mean something to you?"

"Yes… she prayed it every day for me and the family."

Then he said, "There's a man… a father figure… quiet… but he's waving an Irish flag… Is your dad in spirit?"

Pat nodded again… "Yes… that's my dad."

And then… the air changed… Felix's tone softened…

"There's a little boy next to you… he says something happened to his head… he played football… but not American football… he says 'futbol'… soccer… Who is he?"

Pat felt his breath catch… "It's my son… Kevin… he had brain cancer… and he was a soccer star," he said softly.

Felix continued… "He's showing me Disneyland… and a restaurant… Goofy's Kitchen… Does that make sense?"

Pat blinked in disbelief… "Yes… we were just there for his birthday… Kevin was born on Valentine's Day… We celebrated with his brothers at Goofy's Kitchen… it was one of his favorite places."

Felix cried… Pat cried… and then Felix said something extraordinary…

"Kevin's playing soccer in heaven… with a little dog… and he's doing something with St. Michael…"

How would he know this?… Despite the power of the moment… Pat still clung to a quiet skepticism… Mikey hadn't come through… Billy hadn't come through… only ten minutes remained…

Then Felix said… "There's a Michael here… he's showing me a monster truck… and motorcycles… Does that mean anything to you?"

Pat gasped… "Yes… Mikey had a monster truck… and we rode motorcycles together."

Felix added… "He says he doesn't need alcohol where he is now… he's happy… free…"

Nobody could have known that... but still... no Billy...

Then... with five minutes left... Felix looked puzzled... then focused...

"Someone's pushing through... very strongly...

He says his name is William... but... wait... you don't call him William... You call him... Billy?"

Pat nearly fainted...

Felix continued... "He's mentioning alcohol... but says he doesn't drink anymore... He's with your son... says Kevin helped save his soul... They're holding hands... Billy says God has a plan... Kevin and St. Michael are doing work for God."

Tears streamed down Pat's face... it was all too much... too specific... too real...

That day... sitting across from Felix... something cracked open... a door Pat had long kept closed... a truth he had buried... Felix had even said... "They say you have the same ability I do... You can speak with spirit..."

Pat had always known... but had always run from it... this reading... this encounter... shifted his entire paradigm... Kevin was still with him... so were Billy... Mikey... his parents... and Pat finally understood...

The world is far more mysterious... far more spiritual... than most will ever admit... Pat pondered that truth in his heart... and life... though still strange... carried on... with new meaning... and new peace...

33

The Leaf

People talk about signs from those who have passed… little things… a song on the radio… a sudden breeze… a bird that lands too close… those things started happening to Pat…

When Kevin's cancer returned… when there was nothing left to do but make him comfortable… Pat stayed close… soaking in every quiet, precious moment…

One day, they went walking through Sigmund Stern Grove… Pat, Kevin, and their chocolate cocker spaniels…Elvis and Bobo… Kevin couldn't walk well anymore… the tumor pressing on his brain and spine had stolen so much from him… but he was still an athlete, through and through… if he could move… he would…

The trees in the grove stretched toward the sky… a hundred feet tall… light filtered through in golden streaks… and then… Pat saw it… a single eucalyptus leaf… drifting down… floating like it had a mission…

"Kevin, look at that leaf… it's coming right to us."… It twirled and danced in the air… weightless… carried by something unseen… "I'm gonna catch it!"

Pat reached out… missed… but Kevin… with reflexes like a ninja… shot his hand out and snatched it from the air… they erupted… laughing, cheering… like they'd just won the Super Bowl…

"Kevin! That was amazing!"

Kevin beamed… both of them knew they'd just witnessed something magical…

When Kevin was little… Pat used to tell him stories about setting booby traps for Grandpa… Jacks and Legos scattered on the floor… waiting for a barefoot victim… demented? maybe… but Kevin thought it was hilarious… He took the idea and made it his own… his signature move? Sneaking Legos into Pat's UGG boots… Pat would slip a foot in… "Ouch! What the heck is that?!"

Boot off… upside down… Legos clattering to the floor… Kevin would be doubled over… laughing that deep, belly laugh that made the whole world brighter…

He was such a character…

In the last week of his life… Kevin lay on Pat's chest… his voice just a whisper…

"Hey Daddy… do you remember when I caught that eucalyptus leaf?"

His eyes far away… a soft smile on his lips…

"Yeah, Kev… I do… that was so cool."

"Yeah… I don't know why I just remembered that… but it was cool…"

Pat swallowed the lump in his throat…

"You're amazing, Kevin… I love you so much."

"I love you too, Daddy."

Kevin closed his eyes… and fell soundly asleep…

In the days after Kevin died… Pat got up… moved through the motions… reached for the UGG boots… slipped a foot in… something was inside… Pat stopped… took the boot off… turned it upside down… and out fluttered… a eucalyptus leaf… spinning… floating… twisting just like the one Kevin caught…

Pat could hear his laugh… that deep, beautiful, mischievous laugh…

It's excruciating without Kevin on Earth… but the signs from heaven had begun…

34

Hearts & Smiley Faces

After receiving what he took as a sign from Kevin with the eucalyptus leaf... Pat became intrigued by the possibility of this phenomenon...

One day... as he and Dylan were walking up Judah Street... the little guy suddenly said... "Hey, look... it's a smiley face."... he pointed to the ground... and sure enough... there it was... a smiley face drawn on the pavement... then he added... "Kevin makes those."...

Pat looked at him... "What do you mean by that?"...

Dylan... just three years old at the time... answered so matter-of-factly... "Kevin leaves those as a sign"...

Pat stood there... stunned... wondering where his son could have gotten such an idea... but Dylan kept going... "He leaves smiley faces and hearts... red hearts... because he was born on Valentine's Day"...

Pat nodded slowly... "You're probably right"... then added... "I think he leaves number 7s too... since that was his number in soccer and basketball"...

From that day on... they started pointing things out to each other...

"Hey, look! A 7!"...

"Look, a smiley face!"...

"Look, a red heart!"...

It became a little ritual... a quiet language between them... a way to feel Kevin's presence... even if Pat wasn't entirely sure what to make of it...

Then one day... walking alone on the beach... Pat looked down and saw a little yellow super ball... it had a smiley face on it... he smiled...

picked it up... slipped it into his pocket... he'd give it to Dylan and Conor... tell them Kevin must be saying hello...

For weeks... the ball rode around with him in the car... tucked away in the center console... waiting for the right moment...

Then February came... Kevin would have been turning ten... Valentine's Day... Pat asked his friend Bill to join him that day to visit Kevin's grave at Holy Cross in Colma... they picked up some Valentine hearts to leave behind... and when they arrived... they stood together in silence... letting the moment speak...

Pat told Bill about the hearts... about how Dylan believed Kevin was sending them... then he told him about the smiley faces...

"Oh, wait," Pat said suddenly..."I have one in my car!"...

He hadn't planned it... but in that moment... something moved in him... he walked back... grabbed the little yellow super ball... and placed it on Kevin's grave... along with the red hearts...

"I think it's Kevin's way of telling us he's happy in heaven," he said...

Bill... the mystic... smiled gently and said... "Yes... of course he's happy in heaven... but maybe he's also telling you that he wants you to be happy."...

The words landed like grace... settled deep in Pat's heart...

He nodded... "Yes... he probably is saying that"...

Standing there... on Kevin's grave... on what would have been his 10th birthday... Pat made a quiet promise... he would try to be happy... not just for his own sake... but for Kevin's sake... for his sons' sake... for Buffy's sake...

Bill smiled wide when he heard it... Pat thanked him... and they parted ways...

On the drive home... something felt different... lighter... like a burden had been set down... as he drove down Junipero Serra Boulevard... approaching Ocean Avenue... he happened to glance at the car in front of him... it had a bumper sticker with three images... the letter "I",... a red heart,... and a yellow smiley face...

Pat stared at it in disbelief... on that day... Kevin's 10th birthday... something shifted in him...

Wait a second... Is this real?... Could this be?... Did this really just happen?... But how?...

He began to ponder these things in his heart… the way Mary once did… holding the mystery with reverence… letting love speak in symbols… trusting that heaven always knows how to find us…

This life is the dream!!

35

The Cottage in Heaven

Kevin died when he was nine years old... Conor was six and Dylan was only three... they both carried their grief in different ways... but there were moments when that grief broke through in ways Pat couldn't explain...

One day... he was driving down Sunset Boulevard... the same street where Kevin had collapsed on his way to a soccer game... the memory was always with him...

Dylan was in the back seat... sitting in his car seat... eating popcorn... he was quiet for a while... then out of nowhere... he spoke... "I know where Kevin is."

His voice was calm... matter-of-fact... Pat glanced in the rearview mirror...

"Yes... me too... he's in heaven," Pat replied...

Dylan shook his head... "I know that... but I know what he's doing in heaven."

Pat was caught off guard... he kept driving... but his mind was racing...

"Oh yeah?" he asked... "What's he doing?"

Dylan took another bite of popcorn... then said something that made Pat's heart stop...

"He's in a kitchen... it looks like Ireland... kind of like a cottage... with green hills in the background."

Pat gripped the steering wheel tighter... trying to process what he was hearing... this was coming from a three-year-old... and Dylan kept going...

"Kevin's with your mom... she's making chocolate chip cookies... Kevin's wearing Manchester United pajamas... and they're sitting in the kitchen together... he's eating the cookies."

Pat couldn't believe what he was hearing... his mother had passed away in 2009... Dylan had never met her... but he spoke as if he knew her...

"They told me that the life he's in is the real life... and this life... the one we're in... is the dream."...

Pat's mind reeled... how could he say something like that?... he was three years old...

"They told me I can't stay there yet," Dylan continued... "They told me to go back to sleep."

Pat swallowed hard... trying to find words... "And what did you say?"

"I asked if I could have one of the cookies," Dylan said... "But they told me no... not now... I had to go back to bed... I was sad because the cookies looked really delicious."

Pat couldn't help but smile... despite the shock... he was fascinated...

Dylan paused... then said... "You know what the weird part is though?"

Pat thought to himself... this whole thing is the weird part... but he played along...

"What's the weird part?"

Dylan shifted in his car seat... put down his popcorn... and said, "You know that picture of your mom over the fireplace?"

Pat nodded... "Yes... I know it." That picture was the only way Dylan knew Pat's mother... it was an old photo of her...

"Well... in the kitchen... she didn't look like that," Dylan said... "She wasn't old... she looked way younger... she looked like your sister Mary..."

Pat couldn't speak for a moment... his sister Mary did look remarkably like his mother when she was young... there was no way Dylan could have known that...

Dylan leaned back... rubbing his eyes... "I'm tired... I'm gonna take a nap."

Just like that... he closed his eyes...

Pat drove on... silent... pondering everything Dylan had said... he couldn't shake the feeling that Dylan had seen something profound… perhaps… Kevin was in a place of peace… perhaps his mother was with him… perhaps… the line between this life and the next isn't as distant as we think…

Dylan's words stayed with him… they still do…

There are moments in life that defy explanation… moments that touch a deeper part of the soul… this was one of those moments… and Pat pondered it in his heart…

36

The Red Shoes

Every May... at the end of the school year... Kevin's school held an Olympic Games at Kezar Stadium...

Before he collapsed on May 12... before the diagnosis that changed everything... Kevin had begged for a pair of red running shoes... he was so excited to race in them... but he never got the chance... while he was in the hospital... his classmates made shirts that said "Running for Kevin"... it was one of those simple gestures that meant the world...

Years later... when Conor was in fourth grade... it was his turn to run in the Olympic Games... he made a shirt that read "KJM7"... Pat looked at him and said, "The best way to honor Kevin is to always play for him... and have fun."... but Conor shook his head...

"I need a pair of good running shoes because I want to win for Kevin."

Pat smiled gently... "You don't need to win to honor him... just do your best."

Conor's class was filled with talented athletes... Pat didn't want him crushed if things didn't go his way...

Then one day... Buffy was out in the garage... looking for something... she glanced up and spotted a dusty old shoebox on a high shelf... pulled it down... opened it... inside...Kevin's red running shoes... the ones he never got to wear...

She brought them inside... Conor tried them on... they fit perfectly.

The day of the race... Pat couldn't be there... he was away on an overnight school trip with Dylan in the Santa Cruz Mountains... before the race... he asked Buffy to text him when it was over...

That morning... deep in the woods... walking alone... he found himself praying... and then... suddenly... an overwhelming feeling surged through him... not a thought... a knowing... that Conor won.

A rush of joy... clarity... a quiet conviction... and moments later... his phone buzzed... a text from Buffy... "HE WON! CONOR WON! He out-ran everyone!"

Pat just smiled... standing in the silence of the forest... grateful he had saved those red shoes...

Years passed... and now... it was Dylan's turn... he was preparing for his own Olympic Games... and one afternoon... he came to Pat and asked... "Can I wear Kevin's shoes? just like Conor did?"

Pat nodded... "Let's see if they fit."

Dylan slipped them on... they fit perfectly... Pat smiled... but his heart ached a little... Dylan had recently been diagnosed with a sleep condition... he'd gained some weight... wasn't as fast as the others... but Dylan believed... with all his heart... "I'm going to win for Kevin. Just like Conor did."

Pat looked at him... "Just do your best... you don't have to win to honor Kevin."

But Dylan's eyes burned with certainty... "But I am going to win."

The day of the race arrived... Dylan laced up the red shoes... his shirt read "KJM7"... the French teacher stood at the starting line... "On your mark... get set... go!"

The kids took off... there were so many runners... Pat lost sight of Dylan...

First turn... no sign of him... second turn... nothing... he scanned the crowd... checked the back of the pack... nothing... he turned to another dad and said, "I don't see Dylan."... the man pointed...

"Pat! Look!" and there he was... a lone runner... twenty feet ahead of everyone. Pat froze... stunned... there's no way he can hold that lead... they hit the final turn... Ben... Faiz... Henry... Knox... all closing in fast... but Dylan didn't fold... he dug in... he sprinted... he won... he crossed the finish line... and collapsed...

Pat could barely breathe… he looked at the red shoes on Dylan's feet… Magic.

Pat was so proud… his heart… light as air… dancing… and on Dylan's shirt… clear as day… "I run for Kevin."

37

The Stained Glass Gnosis

There was a prolonged time… after Kevin died…when Pat was still in shock… when the world as he knew it had crumbled… when belief itself had become a battlefield… he never gave up on God… he never walked away from faith… but something inside had shattered… his paradigm… formed through Catholicism and Scripture… was gone…

He sat in the ashes of what once was a beautiful, ordered life… still, he kept crying out to God… even if he no longer knew who…or what… God truly was…

Before Kevin's death, Pat's beliefs had been cataphatic… clear… defined… certain… he could tell you exactly who God was… or at least he thought he could…

After Kevin died, everything changed… and slowly… painfully… he began to drift toward apophatic knowing… that is… toward unknowing… he began to make lists… lists of what he believed God was… and equally, what God was not… it wasn't enough anymore to quote Scripture or lean solely on Church teaching… he needed to encounter the truth firsthand… he needed to survive…

Then one night he had a dream …he saw broken glass… shards… scattered everywhere… a hand appeared…large… tender… careful… and the hand began to pick up the glass… one piece at a time…

"What is this?" Pat asked, somewhere between curiosity and awe…

The hand didn't answer in words… it simply began to place the pieces together… blue glass… green… gold… red… each fragment fitted with divine precision…

Pat began to see the image take shape… it was a stained glass window… and suddenly, he knew… the glass was his broken life… the hand was God's… the window was a masterpiece in the making… he remembered that stained glass is most beautiful when sunlight pours through… he knew…this dream was telling him something profound… the window was him… and so he whispered… when he awoke … "Then shine through me."…

Later that same week, while cleaning the home office, Pat came across a paper Kevin had made at school… a simple list of his favorite things…

> My favorite food is steak and spinach…
> My favorite sport is soccer…
> My favorite number is 7…
> My favorite color is blue…
> My favorite movie is *The Rise of the Guardians*…

Pat's body lit up with electricity… this wasn't just a school paper… it was a message… a sign… he raced to the TV and ordered the movie immediately… as he watched it, the messages poured in… too many to name… but one stood out above the rest: *Truth is revealed through allegory…*

It hit him like lightning… not just in the movie… but through it… truth had always found Pat this way… through symbols… stories… parables… it was a gnosis…an inner knowing beyond reason… not learned… not taught… but experienced and awakened…

He remembered then… that's why Jesus spoke in parables… all his stories echoed in his soul… they were revelations… maps… mirrors… and the Bible…he now understood…was no different… he found himself in those stories too… and as he changed, so did their meaning…

One day, he was meditating on the crucifixion story… he remembered not just Jesus… but the two thieves beside him… the soldiers… the crowds… the religious elite… the disciples… the women who stayed close… the ones who ran… and he heard the old church hymn from his childhood: *Were you there when they crucified my Lord?…*

Suddenly... he knew... yes... yes, he was there... but who was he? He didn't want to be the crowd... or the indifferent soldier... or the blind priest... he didn't even want to be Peter, full of fear... no...he wanted to be the thief... the guilty one who turned... the one who simply said: "Jesus... remember me when you come into your kingdom"...

Pat's search for God intensified after Kevin's death... because he knew...deep down...if he wanted to find Kevin... he had to find God... "Seek first the kingdom of heaven..." these words now carried a new kind of urgency... so did the Book of Job... especially Chapter 3...

Pat had whispered those verses to himself many times in the dark... wishing he had never been born... he knew that despair well... but eventually... he arrived at Job 40:4... where Job finally says: "I know nothing... and my hand is over my mouth..."

Pat had reached that point too... he had discovered that God speaks in many ways... through visions... through mystical experience... through Scripture... and now... of course through allegory... through Kevin... through film... through broken glass made beautiful...

He remembered what Jesus had once said: "The kingdom of heaven is within you"... and Pat knew... it was time to stop only looking outside...

38

Ronnie from the Richmond

When Kevin was diagnosed with cancer... Pat started a prayer group at St. Gabriel Church... every Tuesday night they gathered... people from every walk of life showed up... people Pat grew up with... friends from French American School... players and parents from the soccer community... brothers and sisters from his spiritual circles... fellow travelers from sobriety... people from his Catholic parish... Protestants, Buddhists, Hindus, Jews, Muslims, even atheists... young and old... every race... all of them came together to pray for Kevin...

Original Joe's donated food every week... hundreds of dollars' worth from the Duggan family... they created a prayer book filled with their most trusted prayers...the ones that never failed... they even organized a 24-hour Adoration of the Blessed Sacrament... hundreds of people participated... every hour of the day and night...

Soon, people began submitting prayer requests for others...friends with cancer... families in grief... strangers battling illness...

Then one day, someone came in with a new request... Ronnie...from the Richmond...had been in a terrible accident... he was clinging to life... what most people didn't know was that Ronnie had once led the Richmond Gang... he was on Pat's vengeance list back in the 1980's...

Ronnie had spent years lost in addiction... derelict on the streets... a shell of a man... Pat had many chances to even the score... one time he found Ronnie beating up his girlfriend in a van... dragged him out by his shirt... Ronnie dropped to his knees and begged for mercy... Pat, fueled by fury and years of rage, had every reason to beat him senseless… but something inside him…grace, maybe…held him back… it was after one of Pat's spiritual awakenings… he walked away instead… told Ronnie to stop hurting her… that he wouldn't get another chance…

Ronnie cried out, "I'm sorry, Pat! I'll stop!"

He knew Pat's name,… but he had no idea who Pat really was… no clue that Pat had been the kid in Polly Ann's…the one the West Sunset gang tried to jump all those years ago… the kid who had learned… at an early age… that to survive, he'd need to learn to fight. Pat walked away thinking, he's lucky I'm merciful now…

So when someone asked the prayer group to pray for Ronnie, Pat froze… it felt like a test… a divine challenge… was he willing to pray for his enemy?

He accepted with trembling faith… he believed… maybe if he could forgive Ronnie… truly forgive… Kevin would be healed… sadly Pat was wrong…

A year after Kevin's death… Pat was standing at 48th and Judah when he saw someone limping toward him with a cane… it was Ronnie… sunken eyes… frail frame… dragging pain behind him like a broken wagon…

Pat stared in disbelief… no way this guy's still alive… his thoughts turned instantly to rage… but not at Ronnie… but at God… *You let this piece of shit live… and took my little Kevin?... This guy's been on heroin for 40 years… spreading pain and destruction"…*

It was the first time Pat had almost cursed at God… in his head, he wanted to scream… wanted to flip God off… say "Forget You. We're done."

Ronnie reached him… "What up, Pat?" he said.

Pat said nothing. Just shook his head… then Ronnie asked, "You got twenty bucks?"

Pat stood in stunned silence… after everything he'd just been screaming inside… now this?... Without thinking, almost in shock… he pulled a twenty from his pocket and handed it over… Ronnie took it gently… "Thanks, Pat."

Pat nodded… still saying nothing… but then Ronnie added, "Hey, Pat… I'm sorry."

Pat asked, "For what?"

"For the loss of your son," Ronnie said softly.

Pat's heart buckled…He thought to himself… *No. Don't say that… Don't you dare speak about Kevin…*

He was about to fall apart… Ronnie kept talking… said he had so much respect for Pat… for staying sober, for holding onto faith after losing a child… Pat couldn't believe what he was hearing… especially after what he had just said to God moments earlier… then Ronnie said something Pat didn't expect…

"My boy died too… in my arms. I handed his body to my mother, cursed God, and walked out the door… haven't been right since…" He added, "I'll never be okay… but you stayed sober. I respect that."

Pat could barely breathe… "I'm sorry, Ronnie," he said. "I never knew…"

Ronnie motioned for a hug… and Pat…by some miracle…gave it to him…

Ronnie limped away… slowly up Judah Street… he turned back… "Hey Pat… thanks for the twenty."

"No problem," Pat said.

"I respect you, Pat."

Pat stood there… stunned… then it happened… his mind drifted… into that dreamlike state… he heard Kevin's voice…

"Hey Daddy…"

Pat smiled, "Hey Kevin… I love you…"

"Daddy," Kevin said, "you need to love Ronnie like you love me."

Pat flinched… "Oh Kevin… I can't do that."

"Then you don't love like God loves."

"But Kevin… he's not you…"

Kevin responded, "If you don't love like God loves… you don't really love."

Pat opened his eyes… Ronnie was still climbing the block… Pat whispered, "I'll try, Kevin…"

The days passed… and doubt crept in… maybe Ronnie made it all up… maybe there was no son… Pat told the story to his friend, Bill, from recovery… confessed his skepticism… Bill said, "I was there."

Pat blinked. "Where?"

"When Ronnie's kid died," Bill said. "I was there."

Pat was floored... he began to reflect... he realized... Ronnie was him... and he was Ronnie...

"There, but for the grace of God, there go I..."

He had nearly cursed God... just like Ronnie had...all those years ago... and in a strange way... Ronnie had saved him that day...

It became clear again... that deep, immovable knowing... God is real... and He loves Ronnie, Kevin, and Pat all the same... not one of them more or less... they were all His children...

This was the beginning... of learning to love like God loves... Pat started to look for Kevin... in everyone...

39

Toilet Bowl Theology

When Pat returned from Israel in February of 2020… from the Bar Mitzvah of Conor's close friend Samuel… the world was already shifting beneath his feet…

A new virus was spreading… there were murmurs about citywide shutdowns… Java Beach might have to close its doors… nobody was required to work…so most of the staff stayed home…but a few stayed behind…

Pat went down to Java one morning to talk with Donna and Vanessa… they agreed…they'd stay open if they could… young Pat was working there then… Pat had taken him under his wing, mentoring him in sobriety…

One morning, the kid looked at him and asked: "What are we going to do?"

Pat didn't hesitate… he told him to grab the buckets and the mops… and they walked to the bathrooms…

"You clean one," Pat said… "I'll clean the other."

Young Pat looked confused… but he trusted him…always did… even when it didn't make sense… so Pat told him the story… back from Medjugorje… how the Holy Spirit had once said to him: "Clean the toilet… and God will take care of the rest"… and so that's what they did…

Every morning… they cleaned the toilets… and kept the place alive… then one day Buffy got a call… SF New Deal was organizing a city-wide meal effort… would Java help feed the homeless? Of course they would…

they made hundreds of sandwiches a day… turkey, ham, peanut butter… whatever they could get…

Pat took four delivery routes… young Pat took four more… they'd load up the truck and head out… sometimes the shelters would be overwhelmed… people swarming the doors, desperate for food… so Pat told the kitchen to make extras… for the ones who were still on the streets… he remembered hearing Kevin's voice during those days… clear as anything in his heart:

"Love Ronnie like you love me… or you don't love like God loves"…

So Pat looked each person in the eye… with dignity… with tenderness… and silently, in his heart …he'd say: *Hello, Kevin… I love you, buddy…*

Sometimes people would ask him if he was an angel… he'd laugh and say, "No… far from it…" but the truth was… his grief had finally found somewhere to go… it no longer stayed locked inside his chest… it moved through his hands… he whispered to himself as he worked: *AMDG… KJM7…* for the greater glory of God… for Kevin…

He did good works in his son's name… quietly… anonymously… in humble love… what began as ontological shock… the spiritual disintegration of everything he thought he believed… had become something else… an ontological awakening… and eventually… a teleological experience… a reason to live…

As a kid, Pat had been pathologized for daydreaming… for spacing out… for having a "wild imagination"… but in the end… that imagination may have saved his life… because when Kevin died… Pat wanted to die too… his entire worldview had collapsed… and only one thing kept him tethered to earth: he'd made Kevin a promise… to take care of his brothers… to take care of their mama… and when his own life was done… to go looking for God… and to find Kevin there…

When Pat lives this way… with purpose… humility… love… he can still hear Kevin's voice… clear as day: "That's it, Daddy… keep going… you know what to do…!!"

Pat has seen miracles… but he keeps them quiet now… so pride won't steal them from him… he doesn't want to be thought of as a great man… just a guy from the neighborhood… trying to find a way to live… to serve… to stay connected… he definitely is no angel… but maybe he was the one who got visited by them…

40

The Ivory Pagoda

Back in the 1980s… when Pat was just a boy roaming the halls of St. Ignatius College Prep… there was a Jesuit priest… Fr. William Ryan… he taught Theology… Fr. Ryan and Pat got along… not just because they shared the same school, or because Pat had a knack for zoning out in class… but because Pat's mother had told him stories… stories that made Pat look at the old priest with awe…

She had told Pat that Fr. Ryan had been held captive during World War II… locked in a Chinese dungeon for years… years of nothing but stone walls and silence… but Pat's mom said he survived by creating a world inside himself… a place he called *The Ivory Pagoda*…

In that world, Fr. Ryan could make it sunny or stormy… sit on a mountaintop or a beach… eat steak dinners and sip lemonade… not in body, but in imagination… and in faith…

Fr. Ryan once gave a sermon at Holy Name about it… about the power of imagination… about how the Ivory Pagoda wasn't just a fantasy… it was a sanctuary… a sensorium… a place where God could still speak to a man even in chains…

Maybe that's why he liked Pat so much… because he could see that same thing in him… Pat struggled in school… he drifted off… dreamed away… got lost in thoughts and memories and other worlds…

His grades were slipping hard… and if he didn't hit a 2.0, he'd be kicked out… the only hope for a miracle was Theology… the only class besides PE that actually stirred something inside him…

So Pat went to Fr. Ryan and asked if there was a way to get an "A"… maybe an extra paper… maybe some extra prayers… Fr. Ryan looked at him and said… "If you need an A, just ask."

So Pat said… "May I have an A?"…

And just like that… Fr. Ryan smiled and said… "OK… here's your A. You're a good man, Mr. Maguire… just do whatever you do for the greater glory of God… and always remember… the Ivory Pagoda is inside of you… It's your sensorium… it's where God speaks to you… Don't ever let anyone steal your imagination…"

Years later… after Pat got sober… after the streets and the pain and the graveyard of broken dreams… he was living in San Francisco again when a sportswriter named Micky called… the guy was writing a piece on old-school boxing in the City… names like Pat Lawlor and Pat's brother, Daniel, came up…

Micky was a Jewish guy from New York… Navy veteran… survivor of an explosion on a ship that killed the man next to him… he found peace in Buddhism… meditation… hypnotherapy…

He and Pat clicked instantly… Micky started a meditation group called The Tiger's Cave… a space for men who had walked through fire and shadows… and only a few were invited in… Pat was one of them…

"The cave is inside you…" Micky would say… "The mountain is inside you… and most of all… the giant you must face is inside of you…"

Pat got that… deep in his bones… because he'd been facing giants for years… and when Kevin died… it felt like the biggest giant of all…

In 2014… Pat and Buffy decided to take Conor and Dylan to Ireland… a pilgrimage of sorts… maybe to reconnect… maybe to survive…

Before heading to Belfast, someone from Holy Name Church… told Pat he should visit a mystic named Sandra O'Hara in Kildare… Sandra was kind… warm… and strange in that way that only mystics are… she said things that Pat shrugged off… like how one of his boys would play college basketball on scholarship for academics and overall excellence… Pat thought… she's just guessing… these kids play soccer, not basketball…

But she also spoke of Kevin… and of Pat's father… and it started to feel real… then she told him something that caught his attention like a whisper through stained glass… "Your father was a seanchai"… a storyteller… a sacred bearer of lore… at the time, it felt like another thread in the tapestry of his life… but not one he understood yet…

Years later… when Conor really did look like he might play college basketball… Pat remembered Sandra's words… he started to wonder what else might be true… what else he had missed…

After Kevin died… Pat's life had shattered into a thousand shards… and he tried with all his might to piece it back together… but then came the vision… the stained glass window… and Kevin's message through *Rise of the Guardians*… Pat knew then… he wasn't the one who could put the pieces back together… only God could do that… in His own time… in His own way… and somewhere in all of that… Pat began to understand what Fr. Ryan meant about the Ivory Pagoda…

It wasn't a place you find outside yourself… it was already inside… the sensorium… the place where memory, imagination, grief, and God meet… and when Pat stepped into that space… he could feel Kevin again… and his father… and something sacred…

He could hear their voices in the stillness… he could almost taste the salt of the sea breeze from a world he imagined… a world… maybe not so far off after all…

41

Angels as Animals

On that first anniversary of Kevin's death...when Pat and Buffy took their boys to Ireland... Pat explained to them that when saints die... the Church celebrates their feast day on the anniversary of their passing...

Kevin wasn't officially recognized as a saint... but to Pat and Buffy... he was one... Pat didn't want the boys drowning in grief... so he told them that every August 4th, they would celebrate Kevin's feast day... he asked the boys how they wanted to celebrate... Conor and Dylan huddled up... whispered back and forth... then made their request...

"We want a puppy."

Pat's heart sank... their chocolate cocker spaniel Elvis had recently died... his brother, Bobo, was still alive... but cancer was already taking its toll... Pat knew Bobo would be joining Kevin and Elvis soon... the last thing Pat wanted was another dog... he knew exactly who would be the one walking it... feeding it... cleaning up after it... but it was Kevin's feast day... and this was what his boys wanted...

After they returned to America... Conor and Dylan became laser-focused... on one specific breed they had found online: a griffon pointer... Pat found a family in Redding, California with a litter... they chose the only chocolate one... they named her Jojo...

Pat had no idea what he was signing up for... Jojo was a storm wrapped in fur... she tore up everything... including Kevin's little stuffed bear, Aloysius... she shredded the bear until it had only one eye left...

Pat was furious... what kind of sacred feast day dog does that?...

Then came the day Bobo died… Pat was heartbroken… and now he was stuck with this wild, destructive little animal… her energy was relentless… he hired a dog walker named John to help burn off her endless energy while they were at work… but every morning before yoga… before Java Beach… Pat walked her himself… no matter how tired he was… no matter how much pain he was in… Fort Funston became their sanctuary… the quiet hours before dawn… just Pat, Jojo, and the wind…

Then one morning during the pandemic… out of nowhere… a huge dog charged toward them… Jojo, terrified, ran behind Pat… Pat's knee had been bad for years… every step was painful… the big dog slammed right into his knee… it bent back violently… electric pain shot through his entire body…

That's it, Pat thought… I'm crippled… done… the other dog's owner apologized over and over… but Pat waved him off… he hobbled up the hill… waiting for the agony to return… but it didn't… not that day… not the next… not the week after… the pain simply disappeared… Pat started running for the first time in years …

He told his chiropractor Nick…who had worked on that knee for years… Nick was stunned…

Pat just said, "I'm gonna keep running until I can't."

That was five years ago… he's been running every day since… rain or shine… joy or grief…

One day Jojo and Pat ran 15.5 miles together… he called her his personal trainer… he'd wake up at 4:00 AM… and they'd head to Fort Funston… it became his cathedral… because of the pandemic, the churches were closed… the yoga studio shuttered… the martial arts gym locked… even his sobriety rooms were reduced to screens… but the ocean was open… the stars still shone… the wind still blew… it was just him… and Jojo… they would run in the dark… then dive into the ocean together… Jojo would swim fearlessly after the ball… through the crashing waves… they stayed in the water until the sun rose… and somewhere in that rhythm… Pat found God again…in his sensorium …

Pat remembered Kevin's words from the visitation: *Find me in all things beautiful*… and he did… he found Kevin in the pre-dawn sky… in Jojo's joy… in the waves crashing… in his own footsteps on the sand…

It felt so intense… sometimes he wondered if he was losing his mind…

but then he remembered Tom from The Compassionate Friends meeting… and how he had once decided… I'd rather go crazy than live in constant misery… so Pat surrendered to it… he stayed in that euphoric space as long as he could… but as soon as the world woke up… the feeling would fade…

What was happening to him?… he didn't know… but one thing he did know… he was grateful for Jojo… without her… he never would've found this rhythm… this practice… this strange, beautiful way to survive… and the miracles he discovered in that sacred space… were real…

Sometimes… Pat wondered… maybe angels don't always come with wings… sometimes… they come with fur and paws…

42

Kumusta Ka, My Dear

One morning, Pat was running the beach with Jojo… the air still holding that cool hush before the city stirred… and then it appeared… a sunrise so stunning it nearly stopped him in his tracks… the kind of sunrise you try to capture on your phone… but never quite can…

He reached instinctively for his phone… but it wasn't there… he checked every pocket twice… then again, as if maybe his shorts had suddenly grown secret compartments… but it was gone… and terror rushed in before the sand even settled… because that phone… wasn't just a phone… it was Kevin… his photos… his videos… his voice frozen in pixels and time… and Pat had never downloaded them… no computer… no backup… only that fragile device holding so much of Kevin…

Pat had run all the way to the storm drain at Fort Funston that morning… and now stood at Sloat… two full miles away… his heart sank into the sand… he turned back… retracing his steps like a detective at a crime scene he couldn't bear to walk away from…

Along the way, he ran into Mary…one of those beach angels always out walking early…

"Have you seen a phone?" he asked, trying to steady his voice… she hadn't… but promised to keep an eye out… Pat made it all the way back to Fort Funston… nothing… just sea foam… and heartbreak…

He turned back toward Sloat once again… and started to pray… to God… to Kevin… to St. Anthony…the patron saint of lost things… and as always… he tried to surrender… he told God, I place this in Your hands… it wasn't the photos he was desperate for… it was Kevin…

He passed John, a firefighter, and his friend… John said he'd look too… but still nothing… Pat reached Sloat and stood there… emptied out… but something inside him refused to give up… not yet…

He turned around one last time and headed back again… toward Fort Funston… and that's when he saw another Mary… (why is it always a Mary?)… he started telling her the story…

"Good thing we're the only ones out here this early…" she said… and mid-sentence… they both turned… and saw him… a man… kneeling in the sand like he'd been placed there by a dream… barefoot… a cloak slung around him like something from another century… boots over his shoulder… and he was picking something up…

Pat's heart dropped… he knew. He walked straight toward him. "Have you seen a phone?" he asked.

The man gave him a strange look… curious… maybe guilty…

"Yes," he said, pointing vaguely down the beach. "It's way down there."

Pat knew then: he had it.

Pat offered, "I'll give you $100 if you help me find it."

The man agreed… and they walked… no words between them… just two strangers moving through a story neither fully understood… they passed John again…

Pat whispered, "I think this guy has it… I offered him $100… let's give him space."

John nodded and peeled off toward Sloat…

The man kept walking… past the storm drain… too far… Pat hadn't run that far… he was about to shout, *That's enough!*… but something inside him said: *One more step…*

Pat stopped… looked down… and there it was… exactly centered between his feet… the phone… half-buried in wet sand… nearly invisible… he reached down and pulled it out with a suction sound like the ocean letting go…

He called out, "Hey dude! I found it!"

The man came back to him… it still worked… miraculously… Pat pulled out his wallet… peeled off twenties… only had $80… he handed it over, saying, "I'll bring you the other twenty later."

The man looked confused… "What's this for?"

Pat said, "You helped me find it."

He shook his head gently, "But you found it, not me."

Pat insisted, "I wouldn't have come back if not for you."

Finally, the man accepted… and then walked ahead… knelt in the sand again… and started writing…

Pat gave him space… throwing the ball for Jojo…

When he returned to the spot where the man knelt… he expected to find poetry… Scripture… a message… but instead… it was gibberish… but not just gibberish… something foreign… otherworldly… it read: "Kumusta ka aking mahal"… Pat took a photo of it…

He followed behind the man toward Sloat Boulevard… and that's when he noticed… the man left no footprints… the sand behind him was pure… untouched… like a Zamboni had cleared it… not even a plover could do that…

Pat had to know… who was this man?…

He followed him to the bathrooms at the Sloat parking lot… waited outside… but the man never came out… so Pat went in… empty… gone.

Pat climbed into his truck… started the engine… and as clear as a bell, he heard: in his thoughts … *Hebrews 13:2*… Pat pulled out his phone… searched the verse… *Do not neglect to show hospitality to strangers, for by doing so, some have entertained angels unawares.*

His whole body went cold… hours later, Buffy came home… Pat told her everything… how he was trying to decode the message in the sand… she probably thought he was losing it… but then he typed the whole phrase into Google properly… without breaking it into odd syllables… it was Tagalog… Filipino… "How are you, my dear?"

He YouTubed it… and a song came up… soft… sweet… gentle… like Kevin was singing to him from across the veil… Pat sat in silence… and pondered these things in his heart… angels… sand… strangers… and a message from heaven… hidden in the syntax of a lost phone…

Kumusta ka… my dear…

43

Forgiveness at S.F. General

Running in the morning was a great time for Pat to be alone… at some point in 2024… Pat came to a quiet realization… it was time to embrace the dark night of the soul… to accept the cross… as Catholics say…

He began to look deeply into all the trauma… sorrow… shame… resentment… fears… *shadow work*… as Carl Jung called it… he wanted to be free from the terror in his soul… one part of that work was forgiveness…

He went back through his life… asking himself… *Who do I still hate?*… there were people he didn't like… people he never wanted anything to do with again… and that was self-love… but hate… hate was different…

Then a memory surfaced… someone he hadn't thought about in years… someone he needed to forgive… the memory brought with it a wave of shame…

It happened in 1993… Pat had a near-death experience… he left his body… and in that space… he met someone… an angel maybe… she held his face and said, "Everything is going to be okay…"

In that moment… Pat believed her… he felt peace so deep… so real… it silenced all fear… but when he returned to his body… it wasn't okay… he was handcuffed to a hospital bed… arms stretched wide… stuck with needles from sedation… he was in pain… confused… scared…

He looked over and saw a nurse nearby…

"Excuse me," he said… "Can you please remove these cuffs and take the needles out? I'm in so much pain…"

She looked at him kindly and said, "If you promise to be calm, I'll ask the officer outside…"

He nodded, "Yes, I promise…"

She walked out and returned with a short… red-faced… police officer… he entered the room like a storm… angry… aggressive… he walked right up to Pat's bed… stuck his finger in his face and said… "If you do anything crazy, I'll beat the hell out of you."

Pat would never forget that moment… there he was… strapped to a bed… not even knowing what had happened… and this man was threatening him with violence… Pat was bewildered… it took everything in him to say, "Yes, of course… I'll be calm."

The officer removed the cuffs with a scowl and walked out… the nurse began removing the needles from his arms… Pat told her about the young woman who had held his face in the spirit… he wanted to thank her… but the nurse said gently, "There was nobody else in here…"

Pat knew differently… but he let it go…

The nurse introduced herself as Sherry… said she lived in Hunter's Point… Bayview… Pat smiled and said, "I'm from San Francisco too…"

They had a real conversation… something rare in a hospital setting… Pat told her he was going to get sober… live a new life… she looked at him and said, "I hope you do, honey…"

She talked to him about God… Pat was grateful… because he had just been in the spirit world… he thought… there are angels there… and there are angels here, too…

Over thirty years later… Pat was jogging again… thinking back on all of it… he started praying… asking God to help him forgive that police officer… and thanking God for the nurse named Sherry… Gratitude is alchemy… it turns pain into something sacred…

A week later… Pat was at City Sports in Stonestown… lifting weights… he saw an older woman…maybe in her seventies…struggling with a machine… he walked over and offered to help… she smiled… thankful… "I hope God blesses you for your kindness," she said…

Pat told her, "The only blessing I need is peace…"

They began talking about God… her spirit was sincere… humble… devout… she looked at him and said, "You really believe in God…"

Pat said, "Yes, I do."…and then he told her about his near-death experience in 1993… and how he'd recently been trying to forgive a police officer from that night… her face went still…

"Did you say that happened at General Hospital?" she asked…

"Yes," Pat said…

She paused, eyes wide… "That's where I worked… I was on the floor where detained patients were taken…"

Pat looked at her… something inside him already knew…

"What's your name?" he asked…

She smiled… "Sherry."

Pat was stunned… "And you're from Bayview?" he asked…

"Yes! How do you know that?"

Pat just stared… amazed… "Because… you were my nurse that night…"

They ended up talking for an hour… neither got their workout in… but Pat left the gym that day knowing something miraculous had just happened… Jung was right… shadow work… synchronicity… dreams… for those with eyes to see… he wasn't wrong…

Forgiveness was no longer just a word… it was a doorway… a path to peace… and sometimes grace walks beside us… disguised as a nurse named Sherry… reminding us that angels walk among us… in spirit… and in flesh…

44

House of Pain

Pat's whole life had shifted since he quit drinking and numbing himself… he'd been living spiritually for years… but when Kevin died… the spiritual world was all he could think about.

He was a man who had walked through the House of Pain… he remembered being in Oakland Children's Hospital… and at Stanford too… and he knew… no matter what happened with Kevin… he'd never be the same man again…

To see children suffer like that… to see their families suffer… was to enter a kind of hell…he used to run into a woman named Shanda in the coffee room… her daughter also had cancer… she was Pentecostal, full of faith… and she'd ask Pat to pray with her… of course he would…

She told him again and again… "Jesus is going to heal our children."… and he agreed, because what else could they do but believe together?

But one day, the hospital doors flew open… and out came Shanda… running and screaming and sobbing,… arms flailing… collapsing, rising, breaking loose from the people trying to hold her…

They finally tackled her… held her down as the entire family wailed… and Pat knew… her daughter was gone… he never saw her again…

He remembered another time… after Kevin had spent two grueling weeks doing chemo… he was finally going to be released from Oakland Children's… and Pat told him… "When we get home, some people want to come pray for you…"

But Kevin looked sad… so Pat asked, "Don't you want them to pray for you?"

Kevin shook his head and said, "No… if God's going to listen to anyone, he'll listen to you… Daddy, your prayers are the best…"

Then Kevin pointed across the hospital room… at a little boy in a wheelchair, hooked up to tubes and needles… and said, "They should go pray for my friend, Miguel… he doesn't have anyone to pray for him… his family can't visit… they work in the fields in Modesto… the nurses take care of him… he'll never walk again… but he loves soccer too…"

Pat looked over at Miguel… so sad that Kevin was leaving… Kevin was his only friend in there… now he'd be alone again…

Pat would never forget Miguel's eyes as they walked away… Kevin waved goodbye… and they never saw him again either…

That place was the House of Pain… so when Pat found himself in situations that appeared to be normal life… like coaching the boys in soccer and basketball… or simply watching their games… in the world of cleats, tournaments, egos, wins, and losses… he knew he wasn't the same man… he was still walking with Kevin… he was still holding hands with the kids who never got to play again… his mind was on them…

It put Pat in a different dimension than most… they were in the game… he was in the Spirit… and he knew then… and he knows now… that the best way to honor Kevin is to always hold those who suffer in his heart… especially the ones no one else sees… like little Miguel… all the ones in the House of Pain…

45

The Empty Chair

A random thought had crossed Pat's mind many times... wondering if,... just maybe,... he was made for another world... He once heard a quote that said something like... when a person finds that nothing in this world can satisfy him, it might be because he was made for another world... That was a possibility Pat could relate to.

When someone you love dies... it's common to experience what some call *empty chair syndrome*... there's always a chair where they should be sitting...

Pat was a boy who lost his father... then he became a father who lost his boy... he knew the feeling all too well... as a young athlete... Pat should have been able to glance at the stands and see his dad cheering him on... but the seat was always empty...

When a child dies... the empty chair appears everywhere... not just in bleachers or at the dinner table... but in dreams... in milestones... in futures that vanish before they begin... and with children... the memorials aren't confined to graves...

For Kevin... there's a soccer field named after him at the Glens facility... and a tree planted at his school... French American... not just any tree... it stands in the exact spot where Pat would wait and talk to Kevin through the gate...

The plaque reads... *In memory of our dear student and friend, Kevin Maguire...*

Before Conor's games... Pat... George, Pat's lifelong friend... and

Dylan would visit that tree… placing their hands on the bark… saying a quiet prayer for Conor… but by then… Pat no longer believed in those kinds of prayers…

As a boy… he used to pray for hat tricks… and sometimes they happened… so he thought it worked… but after Kevin died… that kind of belief collapsed… Pat began to wonder… *What good is prayer?*

Why would God care about who wins a sports game… when children are starving… when there's war… hatred… mass suffering… and silence in return?… And yet… Pat had seen too much to say God wasn't real… too many signs… too many dreams… too many mystical visitations that defied reason…

He had gone through what they call ontological shock… the moment when the entire framework of meaning you once relied upon shatters… but in its place came something deeper… slower… more enduring… a teleological awakening… a sense that maybe there is a purpose… even if it doesn't make sense yet… and in that awakening… Pat began to discover a single, powerful truth… Surrender…

His prayers were stripped to one phrase… *Fiat voluntas tua*… Let Your will be done…

Through painful hindsight… he began to see the pattern… the greatest miracles in his life had come when he surrendered… like in Jerusalem… when he prayed In God's Hands in the Holy Sepulcher…

Like the day the shattered window at Java Beach became a message…

Surrender had opened doors… lifted veils… worked wonders… so when Kevin got sick… Pat tried again… like Abraham offering Isaac… Pat told God… Kevin is in your hands… but this time… Kevin didn't stay… he passed… and Pat had to wrestle with the hardest truth of all… that even though Kevin was gone… he was safe… safer than he ever could've been on earth…

That knowledge brought some comfort, but not ease… Pat still wanted to see him grow up… play sports… graduate… fall in love… live… Instead… all he saw were memorials… fields… trees… plaques… photos… but no Kevin…

Still… the signs kept coming…

One day… before one of Conor's games… Pat walked to Kevin's tree and placed his hand on the bark... he asked the question that haunted him... *Why didn't surrender work with Kevin's situation?*

That night... Pat had a dream... God answered... *The story with Kevin isn't over... I'm saving him for the grand finale...* and suddenly... Pat saw a stage... a large red curtain... it slowly opened... Jesus stood in the center... surrounded by dozens of children... one of them began waving...

It was Kevin... beaming... alive... glowing with joy...

"Hi Daddy!" he shouted... just like he used to during his school plays at French American... always breaking the fourth wall to say hello... too cute...

That dream marked the beginning of what Pat later called his eschatological experiences... visions of how it all ends... of reunion... of glory... of joy...

He started to feel like a kid who had peeked at the Christmas presents hidden in the closet... a little guilty for his lack of faith ... but mostly in awe...

He felt compunction... but not shame... it was the kind of repentance born of grace... not punishment... tender... not condemning...

So Kevin's tree became a sacred place... a place of surrender... *Fiat voluntas tua...* I will what God wills... as God wills it... because God wills it...

But then... one day... Pat arrived at the tree and found it destroyed... vandalized... broken to pieces... someone told him a homeless addict had done it... strung out... disconnected from reality... it broke Pat's heart... then... came the anger... he wanted to find the man... to make him suffer... to defend Kevin's memory... but just as rage began to overtake him... he remembered Kevin's voice... *You need to love Ronnie like you love me, Daddy...* and suddenly... Pat remembered the words of the 16th century English Reformer, John Bradford: "There, but for the grace of God, go I."...

Pat had been that man once... an addict... wandering the streets of San Francisco... lost... broken... full of shame... so instead of vengeance... Pat chose prayer...

God... please help this man... Bless him with sobriety... With peace... With new life...

The school planted another tree… it was beautiful… but no matter how many signs or trees or dreams appeared… grief still enveloped Pat like a cloak… sadness became his chains…

In the early days after Kevin passed… Pat had heard his son's spirit whisper… *Look for me in all things beautiful, Daddy… I live there… find me there…* so Pat looks… he seeks… he hopes…

But still… the empty chair remains…

46

Collateral Beauty

One morning ...as Pat was running... a thought entered his mind... almost like a whisper... *Look for the collateral beauty*... he remembered seeing a movie once... *Collateral Beauty*... and in that moment... he knew exactly what it meant...

It was senior night for his son... Conor... as captain... Conor stood with his teammates... to be honored before the game... the gym was packed... family... friends... students... community members... all there to celebrate the seniors who had given their all over the years...

Before the game... Coach Paul took the microphone... Paul was a quiet man... he didn't give many speeches... but this time was different... he cleared his throat... and spoke with more emotion than Pat had ever heard from him before...

"I want to say a few words about Conor Maguire..."

He paused... gathering himself...

"I've been coaching for a long time... and I've seen a lot of talented players come through this program... but Conor... Conor is different..."

The gym fell silent... Paul's voice softened... but every word carried weight...

"His talent speaks for itself. He's broken records, led this team, and created moments we'll never forget, but that's not what I'll remember most about Conor. What sets him apart is his heart, his humility, his ability to lift everyone around him, on and off the court. Conor is the greatest kid

I've ever coached. It's going to break my heart to see him go, but I know his impact on this school and this community will last for years."

Pat listened… and glanced over at Buffy… tears streamed down her face… she never cries in public… she's always been the steady one… but this was different… these were tears of gratitude…

The game that followed… was one for the history books… Conor played with a fire rarely seen… shot after shot… point after point… when the final buzzer sounded… he had scored 63 points… breaking both school and league records…

The entire gym erupted… but what moved Pat most… came afterward…

The opposing team's parents didn't leave quietly… they stood… and applauded… they approached Buffy and Pat… shook their hands… congratulated them… "It's not just his skill…" one parent said… "…it's his attitude… he's so humble… that's what impressed us the most…"

Later that evening… Mitch Stevens from the *San Francisco Chronicle* called… he wanted to interview Conor about the game… Conor spoke calmly… humbly… as always… talking about his teammates… their effort… the team…

Then Mitch asked a question that caught Conor off guard… "Can you tell me about your brother, Kevin?"

Pat saw the look on Conor's face… he paused… the weight of it settling over him… he didn't know what to say at first… losing Kevin had left a permanent scar on them all… but Pat had told Conor when he was little… "The way to honor Kevin is to live for him… to play for him… everything you do… keep KJM7…Kevin John Maguire… number 7…in your heart…"

Conor gathered himself… and answered quietly… he didn't say much… Conor kept Kevin quietly in his heart…

After the interview… Pat couldn't stop thinking about the night's events… he thought of Dylan… his youngest… Dylan had cheered louder than anyone for his brother… Dylan faced his own battles every day… living with the sleep condition made it hard to play sports… hard to keep up… but Dylan never gives up… he fights through it all… with courage… with kindness… everyone who knows him loves him for it…

And in that moment… Pat realized something profound… Kevin's story wasn't just a sad story… it was a love story… a story still unfolding… through Conor… through Dylan… through Buffy and Pat… through every person Kevin had touched… his life didn't end in loss… it lives on… in them…

Pat thought of Jesus… some see His story as one of suffering… pain… death… but those who look deeper… know… it's a story of love… of hope… of grace that transcends sorrow…

This is what Pat finally understood on his run that morning… collateral beauty… it's everywhere… in Conor's humility… in Dylan's resilience… in the kindness of strangers who see something special in his sons… Kevin's story didn't end when they lost him… it continues to inspire… to shape… to fill their lives with meaning…

Life is full of love stories… and yes… sometimes those stories make us cry… but that doesn't make them any less beautiful…

47

I Got My Peace

When Pat runs in the morning… he often contemplates mountains… he runs along the cliffs of Thornton Beach in Daly City… by the horse stables… his run always ends with him ascending the mountain… and as he climbs he quietly sings to himself… "Up to the Mountain"… by Patty Griffin…

He thinks about O'Neil's Mountain where the Irish chieftains are inaugurated… the apparition hill in Medjugorje … Abraham and Isaac on Mount Moriah… Cave Hill in Belfast… where Pat had his early days in sobriety…

He thinks about the mountain where Jesus was crucified… Calvary… between two thieves… one repented… one didn't…

He thought about proverbial mountaintops… like the one he stood on before May 12, 2012… before Kevin collapsed… back then… Pat was living heaven on earth… until that moment… when he was thrown from the mountain… and his life shattered into pieces…

At the top of the hill where he runs … there is a bench… in honor of dogs and children who have passed… Pat always touches the bench… says a prayer… the view from up there is beyond beautiful…

The kids these days say, "It ain't that deep, bro,"… but when you've suffered like Pat has… everything is that deep…

Pat looks for Kevin… and for God… in everything… even in sports…

Watching Conor's team play during his final year… was amazing… after his 63-point Senior Night… they made a playoff run… the BCL

Championship game arrived... all Conor's aunts, uncles, cousins, were in attendance... the Maguire's were in the house!... hey were playing Gateway... highly ranked... tough... highly favored...

Down by three with under a minute left... Conor had sprained his ankle badly in the fourth... but he stayed in... there was no way he was coming out... watching his games always forced Pat into deep emotional regulation... his nervous system didn't know the difference between a basketball game... and his worst traumas... that was the CPTSD... so he breathed... surrendered... reminded himself... win or lose... it's just a game...

If we win... stay humble... if we lose... accept it... above all... surrender...

With moments left... Conor and the Jaguars tied it up...

Overtime...

Conor caught fire... even with the sprained ankle... they won... BCL Champs... they were climbing the mountain... but the journey wasn't over...

Next came the NCS playoff run... Conor played through injury... his teammates rose up... every game was a nail-biter... they somehow made it to the NCS Championship... against Alhambra... a big East Bay school... they lost...

It hurt... Pat whispered to himself... *It's just a game...*

He surrendered the loss... thanked Coach Paul for all he had done for Conor... then came the news... they were invited to the State playoffs... unheard of... a school of 400 kids... never before in school history...

First round... Sonoma Valley... they were getting blown out... down eight with two minutes left... trailing badly all game... in the crowded gym... Pat closed his eyes... went inward... *God... I surrender...*

Suddenly... four turnovers in a row... they pressed full court... they stole... seconds left... down by two... Conor drove... four defenders collapsed... he twisted... turned... passed to Jason slashing to the hoop... the ball dropped in...

And one...

The gym exploded... Jason hit the free throw... up by 1... three seconds left... Sonoma missed... Jags win... The Miracle in the Jaguars' Den...

Next came Alhambra again... this time... in their gym... packed house… a thousand fans… Jags led by ten with one minute left… then chaos… Alhambra hit a three… Conor made a rare inbound mistake… the same kid hit another three… lead cut to four… seconds left… same kid shot again… Conor contested… missed… but a whistle… foul on Conor… three free throws… The kid hit all three…

Up by 1… Pat felt sick… *No way it ends like this… but of course it will… it always does…*

Their life always ended in heartbreak… right?

One second left… Alhambra inbounded under their own hoop… a clean look… missed… Jags win! …

Stunned silence… a thousand fans in shock… pure joy on the International side…

Next came the NorCal championship in Sacramento… they played Early Fortune… talented team… thunderous cheering section… down again at halftime…Conor comes out on fire … Conor scored 32… Jags win! Nor Cal Champs!… Early Fortune showed exceptional sportsmanship… congratulating them…

Now… the State Championship… at the Sacramento Kings arena… opponents were from Los Angeles… Diamond Ranch … a school with a student body 4 times the size of International… David vs Goliath vibes… International school canceled class… rented buses… the whole student body would be there…

That morning… Pat walked into Conor's room… Conor was lying in bed… like Rocky before Apollo…

"Hey Conor… you ready?" Pat asked…

"Yeah… but you know what, Dad?"

"What?"

"I don't need the glory… I need peace…"

Oh my God… Pat knew exactly what he meant… maybe even more than Conor did… he thought about Kevin… how after Kevin died… while Buffy prepared Kevin's body… Pat took Conor and Dylan to the park… shooting hoops… all the hours… all the games… KJM7 on their shirts… KJM7 on their shoes… winning on Kevin's birthday… losing on Kevin's birthday… all of it…

Now… Conor said he needed peace… and so did Pat…

That night… Buffy had a dream… they were in a pro basketball arena…she was holding one of the boys as a baby… she looked… it was Kevin…

When they arrived at the Kings arena… Buffy whispered… "This is it… this is the place from my dream…" they sat court side… the student body came flooding in… like a scene from *Braveheart*… the underdogs… the miracle run… the last time the school came together like this… was for Kevin's memorial… Now… could they have their mountaintop victory?

The thought scared Pat… the game began… the opponent face-guarded Conor… took away his 3-point shooting…

He struggled early… Jags trailed by eight at halftime… but then… Conor adjusted… started driving… they couldn't stop him except by fouling… Conor finished with 32 points in the State Finals…

With seconds left… Jags up by ten… Conor held the ball… one second remaining… he threw it into the air…

Victory… Mountaintop victory…

In that moment… Pat heard it…in his mind … Revelation 21:4… he turned to his friend George… told him what he heard… George looked it up…

"He will wipe every tear from their eyes… There will be no more death… No more sorrow… The old ways will be gone…"

Pat couldn't believe it… George had been there since they were fifteen… since Pat's dad died… since George's sister, Annie, died at fifteen from heart failure… George… Conor's confirmation sponsor… always there… every step of the way…

The news interviewed Conor and Coach Paul… Conor shouted… "I got my peace!" Coach Paul said… it was his father's birthday… his dad had passed… it was why Paul got into coaching… to honor his father…

All the storylines converging… Pat knew… what he was witnessing… was miraculous… something in his soul… felt complete…

This is how it will be… we will all rejoice… no loss matters when you win the mountaintop… a foreshadowing of when God's glory will be revealed… when they see Kevin again… no pain will be remembered…

Conor said… he wouldn't trade this feeling for a million bucks… and he meant it…

Pat agreed…

Conor's final senior game didn't end in sorrow… but in joy… and peace… forever peace… Pat would never forget the sorrow in Conor's face… when he kissed Kevin goodbye… but now… he would never forget the joy in his face… and more than anything… the peace…

When they returned to the school… they picked up Dylan from the fan bus… joy-filled… his older brother… a hero… that's how the Maguires roll… when one wins… they all win… when one fights… they all fight… when one cries… they all cry… wherever one goes… they all go… that's what clans do…

After the news reporter finished interviewing Conor… they all walked past Kevin's memorial tree… two little boys yelled out… "Conor! Conor! MVP! MVP!"

They were standing in the exact spot where Pat used to watch Kevin play… right behind the plaque… *In memory of Kevin Maguire.*

And in that moment… for the first time… Pat looked at that tree… and felt no sadness… only joy… and gratitude…

He whispered… "Thank you, God… I got my peace… I will look for you in all things beautiful, Kevin."

Epilogue

Pat has learned so much from standing in front of that magnolia tree they planted for Kevin. Win or lose he needs to take the same action – to surrender, either in humble surrender of acceptance or humble surrender of gratitude; to surrender to what is, accepting life on life's terms, like the fluttering piece of paper blowing in the wind – *Let it be.*

Pat knows there will be many more victories, but also losses – births and deaths, happiness, sadness, joy and sorrow, peace, terror, health, sickness, a tree planted in memory of a lost child, a tree that loses its leaves in winter, and blooms again in spring, a tree that gets brutally destroyed, and a new one planted, bringing comfort, pain, hate, love, vengeance, forgiveness, despair, hope, hopelessness, and peace… but planted out of love.

Pat knows that there are places of surrender all over this world – in adoration chapels, graveyards, mountain tops, valleys, in front of broken windows, and repaired windows, on yoga mats, meditation centers, the Holy Sepulcher in Jerusalem, or in a confessional in Northern Ireland.

And there are places of surrender at home – Java Beach at midnight by candlelight and the first cup at sunrise after plunging in the cold ocean in the dark. Pat knows that standing in these places, kneeling, or laying down, his inner man must do the same thing – surrender! And in that surrender, find a morsel of hope, of peace, and a belief that there is a reason for everything, and that the reason is love.

As he stands in front of the empty chair, Pat must be moved to ask the question, "Is the chair truly empty?" This question may be the catalyst for a continued search for the God of his heart – the true philosopher's stone, and possibly a pathway to finding and maintaining profound peace.

Pat knows the importance of believing in some greater force, a force with an ultimate plan that we will all share in the victory, that we will all rejoice, and that we will all say, "Isn't this fantastic?"

We will then have the tools to comprehend the wisdom of the phrase – *All Things Beautiful.*

A Note from the Author

These dot dot dot stories… are pieces of my life… not all of my stories… Those who know me… know there are so many more to tell…

I want to thank everyone… who has been part of these stories…

Special thanks to Buffy… my boys… and my family… for supporting me… for standing with me in the vulnerability of sharing…

I want to thank Caeli… for organizing these stories…and telling my story in such a beautiful way…while keeping it exactly the way I wrote it … for her support and encouragement… for reminding me that these words matter…

And Kevin Carroll… who I believe was a Godsend… for proof reading… editing… and like Caeli… encouraging me to share what is most personal…

These stories are just my experiences… they are not meant to persuade… not meant to prove… only to offer… in the hope that someone finds what they need to hear…

I have been inspired by KJM7… to look for all things beautiful… and I hope… this collection of stories feels like something beautiful to you… the reader…

With gratitude…

Patrick Maguire

AMDG

Java Beach Café Locations

Java Beach - Judah
1396 LaPlaya Street (at Judah)
San Francisco, California 94122
1.415.665.5282

Java Beach - Sloat
2650 Sloat Boulevard (at 45th Avenue)
San Francisco, California 94116
1.415.731.2965

www.ingramcontent.com/pod-product-compliance
Ingram Content Group UK Ltd.
Pitfield, Milton Keynes, MK11 3LW, UK
UKHW041258281225
9763UKWH00026B/279